- *Is it time we created a world where individı communities are at their empowered best?*
- *Is it about time the world changes its cou... sustainability?*
- *Is it possible that the digital revolution could ring in better days for humanity?*

Possible. The millennials have arrived!

The book derives inspiration from my work and times with the world's most 'scrutinised' generation. Alternately labelled by analysts as being digital natives, altruistic, anxious, stressed, blighted, broke and woke, it nevertheless remains a highly celebrated generation.

Using personal cameos and research the book reveals the why, how, what and what ifs, of all things millennial. It draws from my experience, three decades of experience in raising, researching, leading and mentoring millennials at the university and in organisations.

While the interest in millennials ought to be, and is growing, very few works on them and their dynamics with other generations exist in popular literature. Millennials – Poised to Lead, offers a syntax for this generation when it eventually dons the mantle of leadership of our world. This book is a tribute to a generation which has come into adulthood in singularly difficult times and even so, remains ever hopeful of a radiant future.

This book will help

- *Millennials come closer to understanding their generational traits and prepare strategies for career and life goals to be fulfilled*
- *Interfacing generations like Gen X/ Baby Boomers can better navigate teams and transitions more effectively in organisations*
- *Workplaces and families will come closer in understanding each other*

The exercises at the back are value bombs on leadership and intergenerational dynamics that provide the readers with immersive methods to help steer the transition effectively.

Dear Raj

MILLENNIALS
POISED TO LEAD

For a Generation Who is the Future

Happy Reading!

Mona N. Shah

19/5/2022

ADVANCE PRAISE FOR THE BOOK

ACADEMIA

"This book provides an insightful reflection on the author's own life journey and the changing nature of the generations and their differing world views, values and expectations. Reading this book has been informative, amusing and has forced a degree of self-reflection. Understanding the challenges, opportunities and approaches to life taken by differing generational groups, not just millennials allows deeper understanding of our interactions with them and our own tendencies to curse or fete them based on our singular lack of understanding of their life experience. Anyone in academia, commerce or personal life that ponders the millennial mindset will feel better, understanding from reading this book."

Prof. Michael Riley, pro vice chancellor (interim), Liverpool John Moores University, UK

INDUSTRY

"Millennials were born with dreams. This book provides a lens into the world and psyche of the Millennial, or Gen Y. It is uniquely undertaken by someone who has been at the heart of the vortex of their growth and change since she began teaching in 1987. Mona Shah looks at the perspectives and attributes of the Millennials. Making up 31.5% of the world population, with either China, or India, alone outnumbering the entire population of the US whether you live, work with, or are a Millennial, this book shares the thoughts from one generation to what will be the next generation of leaders around the world. By understanding we can create the right environments to enable that fulfilment. Let's help bring forward the Millennial generation, and this book is a great starting point for that.

Dr. Amanda Clack, executive director and head of strategic advisory at CBRE, UK. Global past president of the RICS (2016-17).

"Eye-opening. Hugely relevant. Inspiring. This book, like the millennials it focuses on, deserves to take its seat at the table. A 'must read' for millennials and their Gen X bosses worldwide! Dr. Mona Shah writes candidly and with great clarity about hugely important macro issues including ageism, solidarity, technology shaping mindsets, social conscience and more."

Katie King, author and CEO of AI in Business, UK

"Millennials- Poised to Lead makes for interesting reading. It is a real depiction of the attitudes, perspectives and outlook of the millennials. The author has done a good job of capturing the millennial characteristics precisely. Their extreme concern for the environment and climate change, compassion and empathy to the less privileged are revealing traits. The contents were so interesting that anyone would complete it in one sitting. Written in lucid style, and lot of analysis, this book will serve as a guide to Gen X and also Gen Z to understand the typical features of the millennial generation. The comparison with other countries also points out that millennials show the similar characteristics all over the world. This book will serve to help in making decisions in matters related to the millennials".

Nixon Joseph, president and COO, State Bank of India Foundation, India

---

"It is insightful and connects with the facts of the fast-changing generation. The topic is even more relevant to us as Indians where 50% of workforce will soon be millennials".

Ameya Gumaste, country manager India, Turner and Townsend

"An insightful, highly engaging, and informative read on the "*generational cliqueism*" that has many interesting narratives. It systematically breaks down the popular misconceptions and stereotypes attached to this generation, by sharing real life examples, backed by data analysis. Mona's personal, often humorous, anecdotal style, creates an instant rapport with the reader. Definitely worth a place in both Academic and Organizational Archives."

Gopika Menon Nair, senior vice president - human resources, training & development - LALS Group, UAE & GCC.

"Create a work environment in which millennials succeed!

In this remarkable book, Dr. Mona N. Shah reveals the Millennial mindset and their style of work ethic, what motivates and drives them at their work place. A very useful book with some real-life examples which one can apply in their business to increase employee engagement and satisfaction, higher productivity and thereby more profitability"!

Nitin Sapre, general manager, Europcar & InterRent, Muscat, Oman

"Overall a defining book on this subject which is so misunderstood. It's relevant for the employer as well as the millennial. Super congratulations on a terrific research based, book".

Cyrus Minwalla, head human resource, Tata Projects, Hyderabad, India

"A lucid description with an in-depth analysis of the leaders of today and tomorrow -The Millennials! An easy to understand blending of research and anecdotal excerpts. A non- stop reading experience".

Madhavi Gadkari, clinical psychologist, consultant and counsellor at IIT Jodhpur, India.

"Very good read!"

Varada Pandit, instructional and training designer, Dallas USA

MILLENNIAL PRAISE

"The observations made by Mona Shah with real life examples of your students resonates, this is what renders a very personal connect and view. I also like, the time the author has spent in delineating the characteristics of different generations. All in all, a very nice read."

Ramakrishna Kaza, associate vice president, portfolio oversight, CIM Group, Los Angeles, USA

"We recognise ourselves in multiple aspects and anecdotes, and we also see our parents (as GenX) identifying themselves with several stories you mention. Some parts in the first chapters are bit more country specific, but still enjoyed them a lot - as European scientists working with international colleagues and having friends from all over the world. We read with both joy and interest the chapter on the millennials from different regions of the world.

Finally, we both consider ourselves as non-spoiled hard- working persons and coming from Spain and Greece, the two hardest hit countries by the financial crisis, some of the analysis others have done about millennials feel(s) offensive. Thank you for bringing them up with an appropriate context and... defending us. We loved and found peace in the end of the book, which we would specially recommend to GenXers.

Rodrigo Bacigalupe (PhD), post- doctoral research fellow, K U Leuven, Belgium and Kalliopi Pervolaraki, (PhD), project manager, Evotech International GmbH Germany.

"Informative, engaging, appealing and not just for the millennials". The book provided a fresh perspective on my own generation. The unfolding of the author's own life experiences makes it easier to humanly connect with the book. All in all, an excellent read".

Agney Das, vice president, JPMorgan Chase & Co. London, UK.

"Mona N. Shah delves into a systematic analysis of the millennial generation: It is marked by miracles associated with new technologies but also great cultural, socio-economical and health depression. How could societal and educational structures provide the direction to understand and convert this generation into the leaders of the future?"

Marta Fratini (PhD), post- doctoral research fellow, Martin Luther University, Wittenburg Germany.

MEDIA

"An essential and important book that gives us an indepth insight into the drive, differences and dreams of Millennials. Dr. Mona Shah has effortlessly and successfully channelised experience, research and analysis into a book/study which is, simultaneously gripping, academic and personal".

Dr. Manjiri Prabhu, author and festival curator and director

"The Millennials are a force to reckon with and *Millennials - Poised to Lead* addresses the relevance of the generation to all. The author's informal, yet crisp writing style and easy flow of language backed by substantial research makes it a pleasure to read. A wonderful viewpoint on life as a Millennial, giving an insight of their perspective to Baby Boomers and Gen Xers.

I found it hard to put down, as it was chock-full of real-life examples which I could validate with some of my own experiences and resonate with it. The book is thought provoking and a must read for every generation as it provides ideas to successfully manage this majority in a working environment".

Nikhila Deo, media content writing professional, New York, USA

VSAR
Vayati Systems & Research Inc.

Vayati Systems and Research Inc

MILLENNIALS POISED TO LEAD

For a Generation Who is the Future

MONA N. SHAH

Published by Vayati Systems and Research Inc

ISBN: 978-93-5416-517-7

Place: Pune, Delhi NCR

Edited by: Punam Thakur

Print Cover design, Printing: Colorcom Advertising, New Delhi

Reprint Cover Design: Prakash Joshi

Printer for second and third reprint: K C Bhide Block Makers, Pune

Third Reprint, April 2022

First edition 2020 Contact the author:
profmnshah@gmail.com; vayatisystems@gmail.com

Disclaimer: Due care has been taken in anonymizing identities to maintain confidentiality. Stories are representative in nature and no situation is specific to or directed towards any particular person.

VSAR
Vayati Systems & Research Inc.

Vayati Systems and Research Inc

To all Millennials -
the Known and the Unknown.

In you we trust!

Contents

Acknowledgements

Generations are links in a chain. The values that shape one generation tend to carry over into the next up until defining circumstances change the sameness of the course. In effect while a few value systems may endure, others are shaped in contemporary contexts. As a Gen X/Baby Boomer and an academic, I have been able to recognize and acknowledge this inter-generational flow through the years.

This book is first and foremost, dedicated to the tallest family one could ever be born into, my parents Shyama and Kamlakar Parchure from whom came not only the penning gene but immeasurable wealth of all things human passed on to me and my siblings. To Nitin, my perennial Rock of Gibraltar. To my own unbridled millennials Pranav, Chiranjay and the cool Jahnvi.

To Dr. Vidya Yeravdekar for providing the foreword, despite being busy 24/7 at the helm of India's most prestigious internationally acclaimed university.

My deepest gratitude to Michael Riley, Amanda Clack and Katie King whose early reviews have helped reinforce the global relevance of the book. To Sean Tompkins who propitiously declared on the RICS Yammer wall in 2019 that he's waiting to read the book!

Huge gratitude for Ameya Gumaste, Nixon Joseph, Gopika Menon, Nitin Sapre, Cyrus Minwalla who read the advance copy with gusto despite their singularly busy work schedules.

To Nikhila Deo, Prasad Barje (who was moved enough, to offer to do a Marathi translation of it!), Manjiri Prabhu, Madhavi Gadkari, Rodrigo and Kalliopi, Ramakrishna, Marta Fratini, Agney Das who in their roles of parents, critics and as millennials offered reviews with care and concern.

To Chandler Bolt, and to my coach Gary Williams both millennials, who make book writing such a lucid DIY activity, only as thoroughbreds would. Thank you SPS launch team for making this one happen for me.

A special shout out to my very own ubuntu circle, which never stops encouraging and pushing me to complete the missions I undertake.

Thanks to editor Punam Thakur for helping with the edits. Hema Singh the patient printer, stoically handling a newbie author, with a calmness that only comes with years of professional adroitness.

Finally, the deepest bow to…

….the thousands of students who blessed me with the theme for my very first book, Millennials – Poised to Lead. Dedicated to those millions of moments with them, pushing my own limits, experiencing emotions I'd thought never existed within me, and in doing so, bringing me home to myself! Thank you all for everything.

This book is testimony that they possess the power to push me to new limits!

Foreword

The book Millennials – Poised to Lead is a well-researched excellent piece of work brought out by Prof. Dr. Mona N. Shah. I purposefully mention 'research work' as I see an academic flavour to this book. This book comprises details of what different generations mean and what is in it for us to understand about millennials; and why we should know so much in detail about them. At present so little is known about them that to many, it could easily mean those born in the new millennium. When we read Mona's book, clarity dawns on us that they were the children born in the earlier decades and who came into adulthood around the time of the millennium, hence *millennials*. Like me, it is important for all to understand the precise nomenclature and this book helps us with it.

She has encapsulated very well the characteristics of millennials in the USA as well as those from China, India and other parts of the world. What is surprising to know is that whether it's the western millennial or the Asian, their characteristics hardly change! She describes millennials to be: tech savvy; self-confident; team players; sceptical; competitive; seekers of immediate feedback; craving stability; fearless towards change; kinder leaders who would like to focus on bigger issues plaguing the world. Very new and rare characteristics to possess, en masse.

This book is for all. Not only parents who are raising millennials but also for corporations because millennials are employed here and therefore must get to know them well. This book is important for us as teachers as there is a large student population comprising the younger millennials that we deal with in our educational institutions. Also, the thirst for knowledge that millennials represent is appreciable. It was interesting to know with statistics that Millennials are the world's most highly educated generation in history.

I would go ahead and say that this book could also be used by policy makers at the national level as India is a country with the youngest population in the world. It therefore makes for a top imperative to know them, their characteristics and aspirations in policy formulation involving them.

I am sure this will be a book that will be most talked about.

Happy reading!

Dr. Vidya Yeravdekar
Principal Director and Pro Chancellor
Symbiosis International University
Pune, India

September 17, 2020

Foreword

Millennials were born with dreams. This book explains how that can be achieved through an autobiographical meander that positions this key generation in a global context with a perspective, that as the baton passes from one generation to the next our role is to understand Millennials better as they are "born to greatness waiting in the wings to soar high." By understanding we can create the right environments to enable that fulfilment.

This book provides a lens into the world and psyche of the Millennial, or Gen Y. It is uniquely undertaken by someone who has been at the heart of the vortex of their growth and change since she began teaching in 1987. With Millennial children of her own, as a self- confessed Gen Xer, Mona Shah looks at the perspectives and attributes of the Millennial, Gen Y, who are born between 1980-1996 and came of age in 2000 in the midst of huge changes in the world including the Global Financial Crisis of 2008. Whether you live, work with, or are a Millennial, this book shares the thoughts from one generation to what will be the next generation of leaders around the world.

Currently the largest living generation in the world (2018), Millennials make up 31.5% of the population, with Millennials living in either China, or India, alone outnumbering the entire population of the US. Due to the breaking down of barriers by the internet, this is unquestionably the generation united in shared values and connectedness. A plugged-in generation that thrives on feedback. Instantaneous and social media savvy recognising the importance this gives to the amplification of their voice. Lovers of transparency and consistency; who will work for companies with a strong social purpose and conscience; as well as for a boss who is ethical, fair, transparent, and consistent; they are socially motivated and have an overwhelming affiliation to Global Causes where wealth is not the primary motivator.

Let's help bring forward the Millennial generation, and this book is a great starting point for that.

Dr. Amanda Clack, Executive Director and Head of Strategic Advisory at CBRE. Global Past President of the RICS (2016-17).

Introduction

This book is not about me – it is about millennials -- a generation that came on this earth decades after I had been trampling on it. You may well question why I am writing a book on the millennials when I am 55 years old. The short answer to this is I *had* to get this story out of my system. The long one is that I have had an extended association with millennials, and feel rather audaciously that this sustained association gives me an 'insider's' perspective on all things millennial. It's like this. My elder son is a millennial who was born in the 1980s and the younger is a tail-end millennial, born in the mid-1990s. Along with them, it was the innumerable student cohorts, comprising millennials, at the universities where I taught. This long engagement with all things millennial was a result of my passion for teaching. Despite my entry into the corporate world in India, I continued the association and was a conscientious campus visitor as an industry resource to teach millennials.

At the turn of the millennium, I switched to a full-time pursuit of education. This was also the time that real estate as an idea was being introduced. The early evangelists of the profession in India were early entrants mainly from the US, and other countries like UK and Australia. I was fortunate to be there at that point in time with *www.indiaproperties.com*, (India Properties Com Pvt. Ltd.) India's pioneering search engine portal for properties. I conceived, designed and deployed India's very first professional certification program in real estate practice that ran all over the country. Thus, began my close journey with academics and millennials, both. In hindsight, I find myself being more similar to the millennials in thinking and attitude, compared to the generation I belong – Gen X and the cusp of the Baby Boomers. It could also be the reason why I did not identify with any other theme but this, for my very first non- academic book proffering.

While on a sabbatical which I took after 32 years of continuous professional service and in my last tenure as dean at the RICS School of Built Environment- Amity University, Delhi, I toyed with several themes which I felt I was competent to write about. There was also the issue of the genre of the book that I could choose to write viz. fiction or non-fiction. It was obvious that given my experience as an academic and researcher, having also served as a visiting faculty in reputed institutions in Pune, Mumbai and Delhi, I would choose non- fiction. Over the last three decades I have been publishing research articles in my academic pursuits, in leading international journals, a couple of trade books, but I have never published a book that was close to my heart.

I kept thinking that a textbook or a handbook in the field of management of built environment was more my thing. It was a terrain long traversed and its contours, well established. But the heart kept calling towards something else. These thoughts crowded my mind while I was living the life of a typical professional, putting in a 12-hour day, with weekends, most times a luxury.

Even so during this period, as is my wont, my mind was not entirely convinced and continued being restless, ending up with procrastinating the actual writing. There was this wisp of an idea that kept appearing capriciously, annoying me with its fleeting appearance and disappearance. Some time passed while I tried hard to focus and grasp this elusive idea and stay with it. Quite serendipitously, in the summer of 2019 while enjoying my solo vacay on the azure beach of the island of Paros, Greece, an idea struck. It was clear exactly like the sky above, that I had intuitively nudged myself towards the idea of writing a book about…. no guesses here…. the millennials.

A book on a generation of people who were born between 1980 and 1996 (Pew Research) is no mean feat. For one, this generation has been in the limelight since 2008 when they came of age during the global recession. Second, most of the existing literature about them has not been very complimentary. Third, perhaps the preceding generations including the Baby Boomers/Generation X were so preoccupied with themselves and their 'greatness' that they have in a sense, overlooked this cohort.

The desire to write a textbook finally gave way to a compelling desire to tell a story.

The story is of the millennials, in the form of a representation of what millennials are in the popular psyche and veritably what they are not. With innumerable personal experiences, and public sources, this book is my attempt to reach out to both the millennials as also members of earlier generations, the Baby Boomers and members of Generation X. This book is a candid offering to serve as a springboard for the millennials to take their place at the table and a gentle reminder to the exceptional predecessor generations to make space for them.

PLACING THE GENERATIONS IN CONTEXT

According to the Center of Generational Kinetics[1] 'A generation is a group of people *born* around the same time and *raised* around the same place. People in this birth cohort exhibit similar characteristics, preferences, and values over their lifetimes.' As per estimates published by Bloomberg analysis of United Nations data,[2] in 2018 millennials comprised 31.5 percent and were closely overtaken by Generation Z (post-millennials) at 32 percent of the total global population (*ibid.*). The generation between Generation X (or the Baby Boomers) and Generation Z, are the millennials aka **Gen Y**. In this book we refer to them as millennials.

Despite the term millennials originating in the United States, worldwide what is interesting is that 9 out of 10 millennials live in the world's less affluent nations in Asia. Millennials living in China alone, or for that matter those living in India, outnumber the entire population of the US. Likewise, within their own countries, millennials outnumber the Baby Boomers/Generation X. Interestingly, in Spain,[3] and Italy[4] the share of millennials is low at an average of around 17 percent of the total population. While countries with large sections of millennials have to deal with the problems of providing economic opportunities, countries with aging populations need to think of succession issues.

---

1 Marketing, Selling to, and employing millennials. https://genhq.com/millennials-gen-y-generation-y-info-2/

2 Jim Leibelt. (2018) 'Gen Z is Set to Outnumber Millennials Within a Year', https://www.christianheadlines.com/columnists/jim-liebelt/gen-z-is-set-to-outnumber-millennials-within-a-year.html

3 Roser Ferrer (2018). 'Who are the millennials?' https://www.caixabankresearch.com/en/economics-markets/labour-market-demographics/who-are-millennials

4 'Demographics of Italy', en.wikipedia.org/wiki/Demographics of Italy

KEY STATISTICS AND CLARITY ABOUT MILLENNIALS AND EXISTING GENERATIONS

In the world today four generations exist. However, some agencies and researchers maintain that there are five generations. Likewise, there could be some differences in the years ascribed to the millennials and other generations. That should not matter much. In this book, I use the term millennials for the cohort born between 1980 and 1994 as described by Pew Research[5]. Though Pew Research was the first to research this generation, the word ***'millennial'*** was first coined by Howe and Strauss in the book *Generations* in 1991[6].

A few cautions to be kept in mind before proceeding with the book are described in the next section.

UNDERSTANDING THE TERM MILLENNIAL, GENERATION X AND BABY BOOMERS.

Firstly, a margin of 3-4 years in the representation of the years does not make any material difference to any particular category of generations mentioned in the book. This is because, the birth years are general representations of the majority of the cohort. Neither is the fact that the person born in these years would be an archetypical millennial in terms of the generalizations of personality traits or the individual's world views. For example, a person born in 1995 may be closer in personality characteristics to a person born in 1997 a Generation Z, and the approximate year in which the next generation is said to begin. Conversely, a person born in 1999 may not have Gen Z's characteristics but may find more attitudinal similarities with the millennials. What this means is that the cohort represents *broad characteristics* as an outcome of the times in which these people were born and grew up and which generally speaking has led to shape their psyche.

There will always remain individual differences within the cohort. This is true of persons in all generations.

---

5 'Who are millennials?' Pew Research studies most diverse generation. YouTube · 18-11-2015 WLKY News Louisville.

6 'Strauss–Howe generational theory' https://en.m.wikipedia.org/wiki/Strauss-%E2%80%93Howe_generational_theory

Secondly, the predominant characteristics of different generational cohorts may vary across geographies because a generation is referred to as a set of people born in a defined geography largely shaped by national and international events that have occurred during that period. Earlier generations were far more distinctly different when it came to their own characteristics compared to the millennials. In earlier times, there were *fewer* events shaping people across borders which were of extremely high impact. Some of these were the World Wars, India's freedom struggle, end of colonialism, and a division of the world into democratic and socialist ideologies and polities. In the case of the World Wars, colonial powers were either aggressors or defenders. The rest of the world was involved as suppliers and service providers in fighting the wars, ruled as they were by Europeans.

Thirdly, the power of international media and universal education was limited. Limited information created more localized impact in the case of World War I and to some more extent by the time World War II was over, due to the growth of print media, education and television. For the most part, it was more often the local priorities, physical resources, and cultural ethos that shaped the collective psyche of the Silent Generation, Baby Boomers and Generation X.

In stark contrast today one sees how the barriers to information have been struck down by the internet. The millennial generation is a watershed among all generations, in that it is closely linked with the rest of the world and through this linkage is likely to question the status quo and demand a change almost always in real time.

Fourthly, local priorities, resources, and cultural ethos have an influence but with an added impact of the existing global ethos, in shaping public policy. The millennials as a cohort are so connected with the rest of the world that there could be comparisons at every level. Consciously or otherwise they are likely to feel 'cheated' if their governments are unable to provide the advantages that their counterparts in affluent countries have access to. By the same token, those from developed countries have a high sense of solidarity with those who do not have access to the advantages that they are used to. Hence, they are most likely to volunteer or raise a voice for social and environmental issues in the less developed economies. This heightened sense of equity and reciprocation was never witnessed in such large measure in the earlier generations.

The world is crowded around the Gen X, Y and Z generations. Significant implications for the world at large.

TABLE 1: GENERATIONS IN NUMBERS

Generation	**Percentage of World Population**
Great Generation	-
Silent Generation	8
Baby Boomers	24
Generation X	20
Generation Y	22
Generation Z	26
	100

Source: Mindstream Media, Nielson Total Audience Report (2017).

It is interesting to note that across different parts of the world, generations overlap due to the varied economic conditions or the political changes that affect them. For example, for China and India, the economic boom conditions akin to America's Baby Boomers and Generation X occurred well into the 1980s and 1990s, long after it had happened in America. In these countries, the Baby Boomer and Gen X's characteristics started being more glaringly visible and their worldview began resembling that of the Americans much later as a result of economic prosperity and a growing middle class similar to that in America. It happened when India and China took active measures for overcoming their economic problems through industrial growth, increasing exports, and investing in infrastructure. Tables 2 and 3 help to understand the generational characteristics that prevail in the USA and their equivalent classifications in India and China.

This would readers to understand the books content better.

TABLE 2: MAJOR GENERATIONS AND THEIR CHARACTERISTICS FROM 1900 TO THE PRESENT (FOR USA)

Year	Name	Key Events	Typical characteristics
1900-1920	The G I generation or the Great Generation	World War I; Great Depression; war veterans given government issued privileges (G I) in housing, jobs etc. World War II; local cataclysmic events; emergence of communism	Optimistic, dogged determination; team spirit; values driven; religious; bigger is better philosophy; affiliations
1925-1945	The Traditionalists or Silent Generation	World War II; grew up in lean times; rations; growth of communism; increase in the birth rate; public education facilities introduced	Hardworking; obedient; cooperative; loyal; large organization employees; willpower; strongest work ethics; thrifty; tech challenged
1946-1964	Baby Boomers	Changing social values; Vietnam war; civil rights; nuclear weapons; world peace movement; environmentalist movement; end of colonialism; emergence of new nations; global poverty increased; rise of capitalism and socialism – hence the Cold War; increase in educational opportunities; women in the workforce; decline in the birth rate	Hard workers; self-assured/independent; competitive; goal centric; resourceful; mentally focused; team oriented; disciplined; self-actualization important; company loyalists
1965-1979	Generation X or Centennials	Further decline in the birth rate; technological revolution; nuclear families; shift from a manufacturing to a service economy; lay offs common	Work-life balance; tech friendly; individualistic; flexible; less loyal to companies; wealthier; skeptical
1980-1995	Generation Y or Millennials	Technology; greatest shared experiences; lifelong access to the digital platforms; always in connection with the world; Great Recession of 2008; less remuneration; late marriages	Special; sheltered; confident; team-oriented; conventional; pressured; achievers

Year	Name	Key Events	Typical characteristics
1996 – to present	Gen Z, Selfie Gen or iGen	Digital natives; world recession; climate change; natural resources depleting; connected; used to a structured way of life; tech entrepreneurship high; grown up with diversity as a norm; social media gives them a 'voice'	Independent, self- confident; autonomous; highly competitive; immediate feedback; skeptical like Gen X; financially focused; want stability; embrace change; want to focus on bigger issues like climate change, life success; innovations

Source: Compiled by the author.

TABLE 3: CLASSIFICATION OF MAJOR GENERATIONS AND THEIR CHARACTERISTICS FROM 1900 TO THE PRESENT (INDIA, CHINA, AND OTHER COUNTRIES)

Year	Key Events	Characteristics	Corresponding Generation in the USA	Dominant characteristics of equivalent US generation
1900-1920	Independence movement gathered momentum in India; impoverished indigenous industry; rise of industrial cities; China end of Civil War (1911), rise of peasant movement; rise of communist ideology in Russia; huge poverty; World War I; educated class leading mass awakening	Traditional; strivers and toilers; conservative; religious; believed in collective strength; loyal	The G I generation or the Great Generation	G I Generation: dogged determination; team spirit; values driven; religious; affiliations
1925-1945	Indian independence gained; Red Revolution in Russia; Peasant Uprising in China; World War II colonial rule begins to end; overall education enrolment increases; women education increases slightly; ideological polarization of the world	Public expression increased; religious; modern outlook; discontent in the level of freedom at the institutional level; collective consciousness and shared goals; strivers and achievers	The Traditionalists or Silent Generation	Values driven; religious; affiliations; hardworking; obedient; cooperative, loyal; large organization employees; thrifty; collective growth; traditional family values

Year	Key Events	Characteristics	Corresponding Generation in the USA	Dominant characteristics of equivalent US generation
1946-1964	Sunset years for colonialism; African nations demand independence; Indo-Pakistan wars; partition; rebuilding the nation; birth of Israel; Cold War begins; half the world turns red while other half adopts democracy	High on nationalism; optimistic, dogged determination; team spirit; suppression of self-expression; bigger is better philosophy; strong work ethics; thrifty; national leadership revered; affiliations	Baby Boomers	**Silent Generation:** hardworking; obedient; cooperative, loyal; large organization employees; will power; strongest work ethics; thrifty; tech challenged
1965-1979	Indo-Pak War 1971; green revolution and food self- sufficiency for India; China begins reformation to end poverty; civil wars in Africa; women enter mainstream; more school enrolments; rise of TV and print media; socioeconomic inequalities breed discontent; growing middle class	Impatient for institutional change; resourceful; independent; free thinking; change seekers; universal values of peace and brotherhood; competitive; disciplined; tech challenged	Generation X or Centennials	Baby Boomers and Silent Generation independent; competitive goal centric; resourceful; team oriented; disciplined
1980-1995	Tech exposed; industrial production increased; highly educated; emergence of terrorism; enjoy material benefits; economic crises in India, China, and Russia	Optimistic; sheltered; assertive; global exposure; ambitious and achieving; connected; independent; want more out of work and life	Generation Y or Millennials	Baby Boomers and Gen Y: self-assured/ independent; competitive; goal centric; resourceful; mentally focused; team oriented; self- actualization important

Year	Key Events	Characteristics	Corresponding Generation in the USA	Dominant characteristics of equivalent US generation
1996 – to present	Digital natives; world recession; climate change; natural resources depleting; connected; used to structured way of life; tech entrepreneurship high; grown up with diversity as a norm; social media gives them a 'voice'	Independent, self- confident; autonomous; highly competitive; immediate feedback; skeptical like Gen X; financially focused; want stability; embrace change; want to focus on bigger issues like climate change, life success; innovations	Gen Z, Selfie Gen or iGen	Mostly match the US generation in these countries

Source: Compiled by the author.

As seen in Tables 2 and 3, with some lags and crossovers, overall, the world appears to be fast converging into cohesion especially in the generations of the millennials and Gen Z in relation to their characteristics. The millennials and Gen Z in the US are more likely to feel closer to their counterparts in China or India than with their own grandparents! On a mass scale, we saw this playing out when the youth protests in Hong Kong took place for greater freedom of speech in 2019, and global protests against reprisals, resonated near simultaneously. In another instance, when there were similar anti-government youth protests in India in 2019, the nationwide university campus' stir was upheld by the students of Harvard University in a show of solidarity for the youth in India. Equally, Greta Thunberg an iconic symbol of Gen Z, resonates with all of the generation worldwide. This is because millennials are the first generation in history to be overtly vocal about saving the natural environment.

Today, youth across the world feel closer to each other as in no other time in history. When mobilized, this connectivity has the potential to bring down traditional regimes and compel home governments to sit up and take due notice of pressing issues like freedom and liberty, equal opportunity, climate change, and so on.

Such is the power of connectivity and shared ethos.

MILLENNIALS IN MY VIEW

I see the millennials as being born to greatness waiting in the wings to soar high. This may not be a popular picture of the millennials, but that's how I have known them and experienced them. There is no denying that like any past generation they are riddled with the same human emotional pitfalls. What needs to be borne in mind, however, is how they have learned to cope and conquer the difficult times and still live in hope of a better future, which for them is yet to come.

This book, my first, had its share of birthing troubles. When I first began proposing the idea to those around me, what came back almost uniformly was 'What does *millennials* mean?' 'Who are the *millennials*?' These were tough questions. If no one could identify with the term 'millennial,' how on earth would anybody be interested in knowing more about them? Rather gloomily, I visualized stacks of my handiwork, my love's labor lying in heaps in book shops.

But deep in my heart, I knew that this is an important story and it has to be told, *regardless.*

Millennials have been around since the early 1980s. Any of us reading this book is either a millennial, or have raised one, or worked with them professionally. I soon realized, by the type of queries mentioned earlier, that not many of us from the previous generations could confidently say, 'We've got our heads around them!'. As I write this book, once again it is important to remember that millennials are the largest living generation in the US, China, India, and in many other countries around the world.

One may well wonder what the millennials are all about. Why are they important for this world? What is it that makes them tick? And why does one need to know about this generation? In short *'what's in it for me?'* This book is *for* and *about* millennials, and for all those who have a stake in a future that we are going to build together. This is a book that draws millennials closer to themselves by helping them understand their own patterns of thinking, their life and professional priorities, the causes they care about, and more importantly, what they do about them. It could serve as their very own 'homecoming', or a reflection from an intergenerational viewpoint?

It is an attempt to understand more about their leadership styles and preferences in all matters of the world. The book will also help millennials and other generations understand the extent to which their counterparts in other countries resemble them, and how they may be different. For Gen X/Baby Boomers, it helps as a steer to all things millennial.

As one who has been associated with large millennial cohorts since the turn of the century and has closely watched their cognitive and emotional frames, I identify with them. As a teacher, mentor, and confidante, I have had the opportunity and privilege to know millennials a little more closely and continuously than most others. I am grateful for this. This book and its contents are like a reflection of my association with the millennials.

A reflection of a significant period in the lives of the millennials. Everyone will find something in *Millennials – Poised to Lead,* that resonates with them at the deepest level. If nothing else, one might get a chance to learn more about them, it's high time.

From knowing millennials fairly well in my career, the desire to reach out to more, across the globe is the compelling truth behind this book. It is the result of those endless conversations and discourses that I've had at home and work over decades, that strengthened my beliefs and confidence in the millennials' ability to change the world. I am taking forward those innumerable conversations that I had with them to an expanded audience.

One can view *Millennials – Poised to Lead,* as a message amplifying to the world, the collective psyche of the millennials. Imaginably so, I would like it to act as a ready reference for future leaders among the millennials. It could also serve as a guide for Baby Boomers/Generation X so that they can understand the millennials better and enable them to devise millennial centric dialogues.

The message in this book for the millennials is that they have to lead this world — molding it and shaping it in a manner they think is right. As leaders and role models of tomorrow I am confident that the book will serve as a guide to help them shape the world's future.

So, dear readers this book is dedicated to the millennials. to all those whom I have known closely and also those that I don't across the world. It is to them that I attribute most of the accomplishments and accolades in my career. It was by serving their cause that I felt the most fulfilled and it was spending countless hours getting to know them better, that made me feel content with my work. While shaping them, I too was chiseled as a teacher. By being a fellow traveler in their personal and collective journeys, I learnt how to deal with my own travails better, and emerged stronger. They were honest critics and strong admirers. They were pleasant and fun, and unbeknownst to them, they lifted many a life's burden off me. Working with them inspired me to inculcate admirable qualities. It was by addressing them that I became more reflective and real. Proverbs and phrases that were oft repeated but seldom taken seriously, took on a whole new meaning -- *practice what you preach, practice makes a man perfect, a stitch in time saves nine, and, as you sow, so shall you reap.* The underlying import of the words began making sense only when I started my career in full time academics.

The meaning of *practice makes a man perfect* made perfect sense when I realized that before entering the lecture hall it was best not to jabberwocky one's way through the session. This generation had information on its fingertips and bowed only to a maestro.

Practice what you preach needed more effort. It required deeper immersion and internal overhaul. It meant I had to put my money where my mouth was.

A stitch in time saves nine had to be invoked so that deferred feedback and it's not-so- pleasant repercussions could be nipped in the bud. *As you sow, so shall you reap,* however, *was* a more distant dream. It was like a fuzzy point, in the distant future for which I had to begin taking steps every single day, indefatigably. It was a somber realization that this was my fiduciary burden to carry. That with every step, I would do my best for my students. A realization that as an educator I was responsible towards society in helping mold these minds and preparing them for the times ahead.

However, it was not always so somnolent.

Those times were entertaining too. A typical day in my life had all the elements of a blockbuster. I was invited to be a part of many lives. Riding a roller coaster of emotions and situations...laughter, disillusionment, being in love, falling out of love, anger, angst, unrequited love, rejections, fear, infatuations, disagreements, stress over examinations, relief and joy on getting a coveted job, struggles with academics, and so much more were all part of a day's work. I went home every day with a bundle of emotions. In those years, I hardly ever felt the need to watch movies!

While I had my hands full with millennial students, I had two of my own at home to handle. The additional sermons, brickbats, and bouquets spilled over from home to hearth and into the hallways of the institution. With the millennials we lived and shared the eternal hope of the good times to come, and worked at building our collective courage to shape the world we were to step into. Millennials were a part of a deep ripple, spreading outward into the world, not realizing then that the water would never be the same again.

For me this book is a form of thanksgiving too. If today, I feel professionally fulfilled and have earned respect, it is through all of them who are in turn engaged in shaping the world, as we would like to see it. Working with millennials was an immensely pleasant and fulfilling experience.

I would not hesitate to say that as a society, we owe the quality of our future existence to the millennials. As the world passes on the baton to them, I will be witness not only to the new world of tomorrow, but also secretly muse the quality of the role I played in contributing to it. I hope this book gives all millennials and others a chance to reflect on how this generation has evolved and how this will play out for us as stakeholders in our collective future.

This book is an accumulation of over three decades of experience in teaching at the higher education level of which two decades were spent in direct and sustained contact with the millennials. During this period, there were thousands of students whom I had an opportunity to address and work with. Today these students are serving all across the globe, the senior cohorts are now in the senior management, waiting to break into the top leadership spots. The younger cohorts are eager to learn and contribute. Many have chosen to be entrepreneurs. Moreover, in the faculty cohort which I led as the dean of the School of Projects, Real Estate and Infrastructure Management at the National Institute of Construction Management and Research in Pune, followed by the RICS School of Built Environment – Amity University in Delhi, more than 50 percent of the members were drawn from the millennial generation, with characteristics no different from the students they taught. Motivating them, imbibing in them the rigor of the academic profession, and giving them opportunities to research and grow as academics was at once a challenge and a pleasure.

The book can also be a source of cognition for all those who feel invested in this generation either by way of being parents, teachers, bosses, colleagues or simply, as curious observers. It puts forth the collective and individual intellectual, social, and emotional frameworks.

The book is in no way prescriptive and rule bound. All millennials are not the same.

While describing the cohort as a whole, generalizations may have been presented, these should not be misconstrued as a 'one-size-fits-all' universalism. For the most part, care has been taken to restrict the generalizations to the descriptive elements that are representative of the majority. Therefore, I have included nuanced descriptions of experiences at the individual level while taking care to present the book as a combination of the general and the individual that will enable the reader to connect either collectively or individually with the contents of the book.

Another disclaimer necessary at this point is that the experiences and persons described in the book are not facsimile representations of real people. They have been suitably anonymized and generalized so that they remain representational in nature.

I invite everybody to indulge me, by being open to the contents of this book. It is at once a bold and humble attempt to offer the world a simple and easy understanding of this brave new generation.

Welcome to the experience!

CHAPTER 1

Me and the Changing world

Ordinarily, no one goes through life thinking about inter-generational differences and similarities. Growing up, we begin with complying with existing norms and behaviors as prescribed by family, elders, and possibly the scriptures. Somewhere, in our young adulthood or adolescence we tend to question a whole host of issues both temporal and philosophical. I was no different. In this chapter I offer readers a quick peek into my early life. My life and career have gone through several meanders which have had a bearing on the larger worldview that I carry. This seeming preoccupation with my wards, which has led me to write a book on them could be attributed to the academic backdrop in which I was born and grew up.

In effect, all things youthful and all things emergent were central to our existence. Both my parents were educators. While my mother specialized in mid-school teaching, my father was a college professor, both career academics, knowing no other profession before and till their retirement. I was born in this family.

Childhood rambles

My earliest memories are of spending countless hours either on Dad's college campus or in Mom's school where my parents tagged my sister and me along. This was the late 1960s and the 1970s when nuclear families were fast growing in urban India, creches were not in vogue and grandparents lived in faraway places. Hallowed portals of learning were places that my siblings and I frequented, as children and young adults.

I remember as a child, sitting in my father's cabin where he was the college Principal, in *Junnar* in the state of Maharashtra, in the early 1970s. The town was approximately 71 miles from Mumbai, the state's capital.

The college had undergraduate and graduate programs in humanities, commerce, and science. As children, whenever we went to his cabin we saw him surrounded by books. Invariably, his table was strewn with papers and dustbins littered with rolled up paper balls, a vivid memory of a little 6-year-old which made no sense to me back then. All those books and all that paper meant little beyond the fact that I attempted basic origami, while putting on an intelligent visage for the visitors. That, the paper balls in the dustbin were Dad's attempts at writing technical articles in economics was fully lost on me. The research that I knew then was only limited to turning over the largish pebbles lying about, or the fallen leaves in the garden to see what lay beneath. Usually, we spied some colorful insects or worms. 'Research' back then also meant a game of hide-and-seek with other kids, running off behind the trees or sheds, calling out the others.

In between the origami and the hide and seek, I remember students visiting my father and their endless discourses. Out of boredom and during the long waits before he accompanied us home, I started paying attention to their exchanges, subconsciously absorbing the manner in which Dad, *the Professor*, belabored through endless queries and doubts. He tackled their counter arguments with a smile as he explained a theory with complicated diagrams and examples. I remember the students always went back satisfied with his replies. Dad appeared to be the only person whose cabin was always busy, not only with students but many others as well.

Somehow, through my childlike spectacles, it appeared to me that it was only *my* Dad who knew the answers to everything in this world! I thought it was a great way to be.

My mother, a much loved and respected high school teacher, served in several prestigious high schools in Panchgani an idyllic hill town, and later in Pune with the Jesuit Conference schools in St. Vincent's High School, and finally a diocesan school, Vidya Bhavan High School, starting from the late 1960s till her retirement in the early 1990s. I distinctly remember the special appointments that parents requested to seek her guidance on raising their children and also better parenting. I remember clearly that this same level of student and parent outreach continued throughout my parents' active careers and well into their retirement years.

The full import of their lives and times, the unending and unstoppable gift of knowledge and life skills that they imparted, endeared both of them to the multitudes of students and families that they came in contact with and whom they counselled selflessly.

Back to Dad's office and his books. Our house seemed like an extension of the college cabin, with unending piles of books and papers all over the house. Tidying the house meant clearing the books and stacking them neatly into the book shelves. In short, our life was, as the idiom goes, *better born lucky, than born rich.*

As we grew up, the piles of books grew with our own sets being added to the existing ones. Like me, any visitor to our house was struck by its scholastic ambience. My father was an economics professor, with a vast knowledge of political theory, history, and literature that made for a heady combination of philosophy and science co-existing in thoughts, words and actions. The world's best thoughts beginning from Socrates and ending with Keynes were fodder for endless debates along with discourses on contemporary politics and economics of the 1960s, 1970s, and 1980s.

In all this, however, the pursuit of the performing arts and sports was not to be ignored. Our parents were accomplished musicians and vocalists. In the pre-independent India of the 1930s and 1940s when my parents were in school, Indian traditional sports were commonplace. In his youth, Dad was a state level '*kabaddi*' champion. Kabaddi is an extremely vigorous ancient contact sport that has found its way into the Olympics and today is played by over 50 nations around the world. My mother on the other hand was a kabaddi, track and yoga athlete. In college, Dad took up western sports. He wielded the willow and the racket with mean facility. Mom also teamed up with my Dad to play badminton and truth be told, I don't remember the pair ever losing a mixed doubles match!

We were three siblings and were encouraged to pursue at least one performing art and any number of sports that we wanted. And so we did. I pursued an ancient Indian classical dance form viz. Bharat Natyam[7],

---

7 Bharata Natyam is one of India's oldest and gracious dance forms. Bharatha Natyam is one of the seven classical dance forms of India, chiefly associated with the South of India i.e Tamil Nadu. natyavidya.wordpress.com/category/

while my sister took up Indian classical vocal music. My brother was a sportsman and a keen debater who won many a prestigious award for his school and college. We could only pursue all this because at home, up to middle school, academic grades were expected to be satisfactory, never exemplary. Hey!! we were not a regimented lot, lest you think we were!

Generally, the emphasis was on being happy, carefree and playful, climbing trees, spending hours doing nothing, or simply reading and hanging out with friends. The poem *Leisure* by W.H. Davies[8] was not the reality of lives of most children in the 1950s, 1960s and 1970s, definitely not so in India. Our own life was not very different.

For most children during those years, it was only in high school and beyond that we pursued academics with some seriousness. The opposite existed when Gen Xers/Baby Boomers turned parents themselves! Wikipedia carries a list of the countries where one parent, generally the mother, tends to focus on the children's academic development with a fierce purpose. Different terms are used to describe them, for example, in the US these moms are called *'super moms'*, they are called *'education mothers'* in Japan, *'tiger mothers'* in China and mothers in Israel, who display a forceful drive towards their children's educational and scholastic achievements. Different societies have exhibited this phenomenon, especially since the 1960s and it is largely associated with the middle class.

---

[8] Leisure -By William Henry Davies

What is this life if, full of care,
We have no time to stand and stare.
No time to stand beneath the boughs
And stare as long as sheep or cows.

No time to see, when woods we pass,
Where squirrels hide their nuts in grass.
No time to see, in broad daylight,
Streams full of stars, like skies at night.

No time to turn at Beauty's glance,
And watch her feet, how they can dance.
No time to wait till her mouth can
Enrich that smile her eyes began.

A poor life this if, full of care,
We have no time to stand and stare.

This growing trend may be attributed to the importance of earning educational degrees which helped improve the chances of one's social and professional mobility.

GROWING WITH BOOKS

Going back to my life growing up, I recollect distinctly that for students who were under my parents' tutelage our house was always home. Mom never complained when Dad, without prior notice, invited his students to partake of meals. My siblings and I were expected to lend her a helping hand. If we complained because our personal schedules were disrupted, we were always reminded that spreading knowledge was like doing charity and therefore had to be done with utmost selflessness and least complaint. According to my parents, it was not good practice to turn away students who came to seek knowledge. So, you can imagine our home as an open house for all who sought unfettered discussions or deep insights, regardless of their station. Many would come to simply listen in case they were not up to participating in such 'free thinking' forums; nonetheless all went back much the wiser.

And in the meanwhile, unbeknownst to anybody back then, Dad and Mom seemed to be collecting their own fan club.

I recall one incident. As a family, we were on a weekend trip in the countryside around Junnar, the town where my Dad served as the college Principal. Dad had a jalopy of a car, into which he bundled the family for these short outings. The car, a 1950 Ford, was like our very own Herbie which very often went 'bananas'. With her own mind and moods, on this particular trip, the car decided she'd had too much of everything. Well, she abruptly decided to break down (or should we say decided upon taking some rest?), in the middle of nowhere, in the middle of the night! We found ourselves on a rundown village road, that disappeared into the inky silent darkness!

Quite a predicament! Complete darkness, a lonely country road with no sign of life after sundown. That was the age of no mobile phones, hardly any cars and almost non- existent electricity and phone service in rural India. After a lot of torchlight tinkering by my Dad and brother, we began to feel a sense of the inevitable. Mom quietly began preparing us for spending the night in the car and feeding us from surplus food cache in the picnic hamper. As you may have guessed, it was going to be an adventure, and she was prepared.

Being the baby in the family I was the first to fall asleep. I was abruptly awakened by animated voices and happy laughter outside the car. The rest of the proceedings are a bit fuzzy and all I remember of the incident now, is that we soon found ourselves in another larger, well-appointed car.... like a van, and on our way to somewhere. Dad was sitting beside the person who was taking us in his car and both of them were talking and laughing. Many years later when I shared the incident with my parents, I was told that that the good Samaritan was Dad's former student. He was the now the magistrate of the district (DM). A man who wielded judicial power and considerable clout.

It was after his customary visit around the countryside on his way home that the DM spotted us stranded on the road. When he saw a car parked on the side of the road, he slowed down to find out who it was, Dad continued describing the incident. As he drew closer, it struck him that something about the car was oddly familiar. He peered at the car's number plate and model. He told my Dad that as he drew nearer, in the beam of his car's lights our car resembled the car in the popular 1960s movie *Chitty Chitty Bang Bang,* a secret sobriquet that Dad's students had coined for our car. It seemed like a *déjà vu* seeing the car there and that was the reason he stopped his car.

Dad's former student had graduated and cleared the civil services examination to become quite a powerful functionary in the state bureaucracy. The rest of the night and the following day were spent being looked after rather solicitously. Later in the evening we were back on our way after our jalopy was repaired.

It was clear however, that the power of his love and respect for his former professor had not diminished, despite the upward trajectory of his career.

The implications of this connectedness could not have dawned on me as a child. It was only decades later, after I had made the transition from the corporate world to academia, that these implications truly came home.

In school, I brought home tacky records in academics. I graduated from high school with decent but not distinctive grades. It was only in college, that I did well in academics in the early decade of the eighties studying economics, with minors in political science and history at Fergusson College, Pune. My Dad had taken up a post in Fergusson College. Fergusson College is one of the oldest institutions in India, which was established in 1885 by enlightened freedom fighters and social reformists like B.G. Tilak, G. G. Agarkar, and Vishnushastri Chiplunkar. To this day Fergusson College is ranked in the top five graduate colleges in India for its scholastic contributions to society. This college has hundreds of distinguished alumni and has produced two Prime Ministers, several Chief Ministers of states and a galaxy of scientists, economists, litterateurs, performing artists and so on, in its 135 years of existence.

At Fergusson College, I went on to win many scholarships and awards as a meritorious student. Something had changed for the carefree, happy go lucky girl of yore. Was it that I'd found my mojo?

ADOLESCENT NARRATIVES

In the decades of the 1950s-1970s, our elders expected us to seek opportunities for developing our personalities in wholesome ways. In fact, there was huge emphasis on this. This meant discovering pursuits apart from the scholarly. It entailed scrambling for subscriptions to clubs that were meant to encourage a variety of skills or serve as platforms of evocation or simply as places that fulfilled our deepest desires.

It was in this period that adolescence hit me and all of my ilk and we went forth in pursuit of freedom and liberty with unadulterated gusto. Those were the times of the Beatles, Che Guevara, Bob Dylan, Rolling Stones, Ruth Badie Ginsburg, and Flower Power in the late 1960s and 1970s. Those were times of iconic sportsmen like Bjorn Borg, Muhammad Ali, Nadia Comeneci, Sunil Gavaskar, Michael Holding, Mark Spitz, Franz Beckenbauer, and Chris Evert. We in India, watched them on blurry black and white TV sets, plying their exquisite craft.

These individuals were so great that they redefined their particular field with their signature styles and iconic achievements.

The age of independent thinking, freedom of speech, of standing up against apartheid, social and economic inequalities and other ills, became the new religion lapped up avidly by the youth. Rebellion was normal. To rebel was to underscore that we loved our freedom over all else. We could think independently, upholding liberal ideals as our core. In all this, each one of us was on our own journey of self-discovery. Pushing our limits was a way of proving our capabilities to our elders, the Silent Generation.

Little wonder then, that I found myself in a serious mode of self-discovery. While hanging out with peers in small groups and looking at the world with nonchalance, I did secretly think about life and the way I'd want to shape it. The external portrayal of being cool did little to hide the fierce ambitions that lay beneath. Within, was a person waiting to live life to the fullest, waiting to spread my wings and take flight. With this strong internal stimulus, I sought to develop every aspect of my personality through sports, cultural engagement, volunteering, and student politics.

I started participating in sports competitions, performing arts, quizzes, debates, and also organized many events. I successfully ran for elections, and held the post of the class leader in the freshman, sophomore, and junior years in college. In the senior year, I ran for elections and was chosen to lead the entire student body as its joint president. It was an excellent opportunity to collaborate with peers and learn to solve problems while leading our teams in inter-college tournaments. This body represented approximately 4,000+ students in 1985. It was an iconic year when the college was also celebrating its centenary.

This gave the student committee an opportunity to start new initiatives in the college. We decided to organize a massive student cultural fest. The scale was huge as our committee had decided to invite fellow students from many colleges in India. This fest gave our student committee deep insights into motivation and leading teams. And new learning too. Through the fest we intended to burst on the national scene, showing to the whole of India what this 100-year-old institution was all about, collective adrenaline ran high. As one leading the committee, with our team of office bearers, required new lessons in empathy to understand rival opinions, handling crowds, performers, competitors, rival college groups and so on. For any student of the time, being active in curricular and extra-curricular engagements was considered a cornerstone of being shaped into leadership positions in one's later years. And we were getting just the experience we needed.

In all these growing up influences and activities there existed a simultaneous juxtaposition of politics and economics playing out in India which had a large bearing on our thought.

The late 1970s and 1980s were turbulent times in India. Unemployment was rampant and the feisty woman Prime Minister of India, Indira Gandhi paid for it with her life. Militant labor unions were calling shots, as factory after factory was being shut down. To add to it, computers were being introduced in the country and there were long drawn agitations over fears it would add to the existing unemployment. The Indian economy was not in its best shape. The government was not very stable and there was general gloom with respect to growth prospects. Those who did not possess inherent talent and education had to toil relentlessly to acquire proficiency.

All was not fun and frolic or peaceful for adolescents back then. Our hands were full with building personal competencies while taming our raging hormones. The pressure to acquire skills to compete in a turbulent world continued to be far too intense.

A NEW ENTRANT IN THE BUSINESS WORLD

As mentioned earlier, computers were invading traditional jobs and the employment market was tight. In those trying times, we were reminded by our elders that there was always room for the competent and the erudite. In this intense competition, we found that our peers were giving it their all to get admitted to stellar institutions. It was not enough to have good grades, one needed to show more talent, medals, and trophies even to be noticed, let alone qualify.

It was dubbed by the World Bank as 'jobless growth' in the 1980s. Organized labor had become quite vociferous in its demands for fair wages and benefits. The most common practices for non- cooperation was to declare strikes, or 'go slow', or do 'tools down' to decrease productivity. Valuable man-days of work were lost leading to a grim situation of perpetual unpredictability.

On the other side, employers expected near complete *kowtowing* from their employees. From USA in the West to Japan in the East, the circumstances did not vary. It was common to spend long hours at work, play golf on Sundays, ask for favors, tipple with the boss or workplace associates, and keep an ear on office gossip. It was considered 'fair' to resort to 'street smart' solutions as they were referred to. All this was to keep the bottom line healthy and profits growing.

The modern-day version of monarchy was the Wall Street and its equivalents across the world. *Grow Big, Produce More, Sell More,* and then *Grow Even Bigger, Produce Even More, and Sell Even More* was the name of the game. Commensurately, this was the very world that held a lot of promise and anticipation for the typical urban youth like me, with top-drawer education, impatient to achieve social and economic mobility.

For executives working in corporations, the common corporate mantra was to play big and play hard. In B-schools, where one aspired to learn the ropes of doing business and acquiring a cool lifestyle, the teaching was skewed in favor of the iconic. In the 1980s and 1990s some icons that were worshipped were Charles Kemmons Wilson of Holiday Inn, Ray Kroc of McDonalds, Henry Ford of Ford Motors, Richard Branson of Virginia Group, and of course, the great millionaire investor Warren Buffett. Diabolically so, even Ivan Boesky, Bernard Madoff of USA, and the Indian Manu Chhabria had a large following among the youth despite their questionable credentials as rogue investors. These names brought down the Wall Street in the early 1990s with their unethical trading practices and hostile takeover bids of perfectly well-run corporations. In those times, they were inadvertently idolized as *successful businessmen*.

It was also in these times, that a large cohort of Gen X had stepped into adulthood.

For Gen X, B-school portals beckoned and were preferred milestones in one's career path. We were constantly urged to believe that if we felt we were the best, and thought we could make a difference, a B-school was the place to be in. Furthermore, a B-school degree meant we got to solve *real* problems and lead *real* teams.

Soon I found myself toiling away to get admitted into a top B-school. I also made it into one.

I was admitted to the reputed Symbiosis Institute of Business Management (SIBM) in Pune. SIBM is ranked among the top-10 B-schools in India and has alumni spread globally, in eminent corporations and in top roles. The institution was founded by an academic visionary Dr. S.B. Mujumdar who pioneered affordable world class education in India in the 1970s based on exemplary tenets of excellence, dynamism and interdependence. The institute provided a breeding ground for the formation of our expanded worldviews and desire to soar high. The selection process was conducted with a special bias to unearthing those with a track record of achievements, experience, leadership orientation and entrepreneurial talent.

With the best of Indian and international talent under the same roof classroom discussions had experiences pouring in from several geographies. The two years there, were a study in human behavior and personal growth, pitting ourselves against highly captious and competitive mates. It was also a great fun place where learning coexisted with a spirit of competition and close camaraderie.

To all of us, it opened a window to the world, like no other.

Armed with a master's degree in management, I had already entered the world of business and was enjoying the material benefits of a leading alma mater and fine professional qualifications. For me, it had opened the doors to a world of success and adventure.

THE GRADUATION DAY SURPRISE

Interestingly, the day I received my degree, my Dad, looking over his reading glasses, casually asked me when I would find the time to pursue a doctoral degree. Can you imagine my reaction? I stared at him in disbelief, completely dumbstruck. Here I was a freshly minted MBA, on the threshold of a long career, looking forward to a life of freedom from books and academic humdrum, stepping into the real-world. Here I was dreaming of being the head honcho of a large firm, achieving enviable success in business and in so doing my family proud.

My mouth remained wide open while all these thoughts whirred through my mind.

How could he possibly think of suggesting this, when all I wanted was to end further studies and get on with my life? Wasn't a master's degree good enough for him? Wasn't he happy that his daughter was a well-qualified, independent woman with a job in her pocket, even before she'd stepped out of the campus? Apparently not! The only prosperity he knew of was, *knowledge*. I glanced at him and sighed inwardly at his naivete.

The years at business school, the intense competition that I had gone through, had changed me from within. He failed to see that gone was his young daughter, now replaced by a confident, highly ambitious person whose primary purpose at that point in time was to succeed in the corporate world.

It is therefore a foregone conclusion that I was not to be convinced and made it amply clear to him. I must've sounded rather impatient when I explained to him that the adrenaline of action was waiting for me and there was no way he was going to put a spoke in my onward march.

Soon enough, I left Pune and took up board in one of India's largest metropolitan cities which is the heart of business too, Mumbai. Well, soon enough, the whirligig of corporate life engulfed me and asserting my identity became my new mantra. What mattered was how fast I was edging my way up the organizational hierarchy vis-a-vis my peers. It was a good life; hedonistic, materially satisfying, and fast paced; there was no time to think. As days went by, my past began to seem distant and hazy and so did Dad's suggestion of pursuing a higher degree.

Not much changed in my family. All the academics in the household (by this time, my brother and his spouse had decided to pursue careers in research and academic), continued in much the same way as earlier. All were busy researching, teaching courses in their respective fields and writing textbooks for the next generation. At that time, I never ceased to wonder how my parents kept alive the flame of knowledge despite their advancing years.

Looking back, I realize that the greatest beneficiary of their work, was the next generation. When my children – the millennials were growing up, like me, they too got a childhood greatly influenced by their grandparents, albeit intermittently. I found it was almost similar in other households where either parent or both were academics.

For most millennials, it was a childhood steeped in creativity and discovery. It was made of endless discourses between grandparents and children about all things abstract and temporal. Every question which we as parents' side stepped was treated with gravitas by the grandparents. Our high- pressure corporate lifestyles left us with little time and patience. Definitely curiosity was encouraged, there were open discussions on any topic that had caught the kids' fancy. Like their own parents had been before them, millennials kids were encouraged to question while also being nudged to find answers. Most of the grandparents belonged to the Greatest Generation.

For me and for most of my generation, life continued in an endless circle of hard work, weekends with kids, catching up on chores, socializing, and back to a new work week. Our lives were typical of most urban households. As parents, we spent most weekends negotiating the following week's schedules around school work, leisure activities, and other pursuits. The children grew up pretty much independently except for the landline telephone that kept them linked to their grandparents, the extended family and friends.

However, somewhere in the future, this changed for me.

CHAPTER 2

The Bend in The Road

A decade and a half went by in corporate life, when an unfamiliar void began to creep in. Feelings of having an empty existence and guilt about leading a 'selfish' life started taking hold of me. There was a constant yearning to accomplish something more substantial and meaningful in contrast to the life I had been leading till then. For many years this feeling was suppressed in pursuit of the material and mundane. In rare, listless moments, discontent made its presence felt strongly. Over time, the same thought kept coming back more frequently. Pushing it away, gradually gave way to accepting it and later mulling over it.

Those long months of mulling and addressing the reason behind the void led to the discovery that there was something substantial and significant that was missing in my kids' world. Thoughts became clearer and it dawned on me that it was the love of books and the time spent with them, that was clearly missing in their lives. Despite the spells of time spent with grandparents, for the most part, I could see that my kids were increasingly drawn to the television and computer screens.

Theirs was not a world of imagination but of stark realism. With their friends they shared thoughts of the mundane. The essays they wrote at school were drab because of their limited vocabulary and were painfully devoid of originality or imagination. They were fast falling victim to the encapsulated, prescriptive world of classroom learning.

What also did not help were the increased distractions with mobile phones and all things accompanying them. It was as if the instrument had supernatural powers to hold the whole millennial generation in thrall. Watching them day by day, convinced me that losing ground to this teeny-weeny gadget would never find favor with me. So, I decided to declare my very own private war against it.

I soon found that the only way out was for me to confront my own goals in life. The moot point being whether I was going to be happy earning material wealth and success at the cost of handing over the responsibility of shaping my children's life to some *-thing* else? Education in my formative years had been richly supplemented by discourse and debate. Mere thoughts were like clay yet when shaped by veterans, it had made me a wholesome individual.

Such was the draw of our childhood conditioning that my chosen profession and its incumbent comforts no longer meant anything to me. The thought of pursuing knowledge and dedicating myself to it, started giving me solace and I decided to do something about it.

After a long and intense struggle with myself, and following a somber discussion with my family and parents, I decided to quit the world of business to pursue the life of an academic. This was around the turn of the century, the beginning of the new millennium. I moved into an academic career and enrolled myself in a part time doctoral program. Thus, began my life as an academic, in other words, a life of an ascetic. Or almost!

Gone overnight were the fat earnings and carefree indulgences. It was back to the modest lifestyle of my childhood. For me, it was almost like going back to the basics, while immersing myself in the world of knowledge and profound thoughts. The midnight oil started burning bright. Complex concepts and theories that had been pushed deep into the recesses of the mind. had to be brought to the fore. This time around, the relative passivity of being a student gave way to a didactic pursuit of knowledge. The lens had changed completely. It was back to school, back to books, back to classrooms, back to being among the young and restless. All the time- tested books in management were fished out — Koontz & O'Donnell for management theory, Philip Kotler for marketing management, Gary Dressler for human resource management, Michael Porter for strategic management and other tomes of real estate literature.

Real estate as an idea and organized industry had finally reached the Indian business scene. However, there was a serious dearth of home-grown academic literature and research available to identify with contextual situations. Incidentally my stint in the Indiaproperties.com education vertical had got me intrigued by the subject. I decided to pursue a doctoral research in it. I decided to work single handedly to apply my intellectual abilities in developing the requisite literature to the domain of real estate and related areas like urban infrastructure, sustainability project management and so on.

RAISING MILLENNIALS AT HOME AND WORK

Easing into the shift away from corporate life to my new life, it was time to pay quality attention to the millennials at home. With my *'born again'* scholastic pursuits duly reinstated, I started noticing their improved response to learning. There was a palpably higher interest in absorbing the learning received in school, as well as out of it. The contrast from earlier times was more apparent when questions related to Shakespeare, Byron, relativity, or gravity, started assuming greater significance compared to Pokemon or Johnny Bravo cartoons. I happily noticed in them a newfound interest in wanting to know more.

Interestingly, while serving in the school parents' association, I came across parents declaring their increasing inability to keep their children away from screens of all kinds. They waxed eloquent about one particular small screen. In the decade preceding the millennium, this new screen was far less ubiquitous. This screen was far smaller than the television and personal computer or laptop but it kept children and also infants riveted to it. It was the screen of the mobile (cell) phone. Perhaps the inbuilt trick was that it could be held in the palm of a small hand and brought as close as one would like to be able to read and watch the content. That was what made kids go wild with their mobile screens.

They were so close and personal, exactly like the toys! Even a child could establish an unbreakable relationship with it. I saw kids clutching on to their parents' cell phones practically everywhere one encountered them -- in parks, malls, in transit, and even inside homes. I also saw how difficult it was for us to tear them away from the gadget.

While I was observing this phenomenon grow all around me, there were also growing plaints by parents and teachers. Going by the nature of these complaints, it turned out that this particular screen was emerging as the most intrusive and unstoppable entity in the lives of school children. The collateral effect of this phenomenon was an alleged lowered concentration and focus and far lower interest in scholastic pursuits among children. Such a statement may appear sweeping and arbitrary, yet the two most prominent entities in a child's growing up years, parents and teachers -- are generally the quickest to grasp even the subtlest of changes in children. The mobile screen had somehow not only caught the fancy of the millennial generation but it also seemed to have strange magical powers to permeate their entire beings.

Around the world, in the two decades preceding the millennium, the advent of the personal mobile phone and the Internet, is recorded as the most paradigmatic change of modern times.

The mid-1980s and early 1990s was also the time when the first cohort of millennials had started studying in school. Computers and mobiles brought about an irreversible change in the way the children received education much like what TV screens had done to the earlier generation. It was simply a matter of time when sophisticated software and device integration enabled the modest in size mobile screens to be loaded with the internet, games, and entertainment. In this scenario who could believe that there was no change in the world? Such was the potency of this disruption that the world had inexorably and irreversibly changed.

As years went by, the world wide web supplanted the traditional knowledge providers, the teachers. In classrooms, one witnessed a creeping change. A certain air of self-assurance, a cockiness, and an easy irreverence was directed at once towards all three pillars of learning -- the curriculum, the delivery of content, and the teacher who imparted the learning. This was in stark contrast to my school days. As a generation, we believed that a teacher spoke the god's word and was seldom to be challenged. The teacher carried an aura that glowed into our homes and parents had to comply with the teacher's advice.

Such exultation was somehow lost in transit by the time the early cohorts of millennials came out of school. A growing number of urban households had both parents working and the loss of reverence could also be attributed to us, as parents of millennials. In the rough and tumble of our lives, the demanding routines had already affected the parents' ability to provide the same extent of *'at home'* attention that we received as children from our *'stay-at-home'* mothers.

Willy-nilly, more millennial children than earlier generations were latch key kids, independent in many ways yet closely monitored. They were kids who received detailed instructions coupled with intermittent phone calls or little post-its memos stuck on the refrigerator. Millennial children were sent for after-school activities and were almost always accompanied by other kids with similar lifestyles.

Parents bent over backwards to ensure that their kids received the very best of everything, regardless of their station in life. They invariably received the best instruction, best opportunities, and well-rounded development. Only what was at a premium was time. Urban millennials had to make do with less of their parents' time and attention.

It was no surprise that the extent and depth of parental influence that I had received, and as most kids in my time did, was diminishing rapidly. As parents, most of us struggled in dealing with a school mate who had access to search engines such as Inktomi, Yahoo! and the likes, which dished out informational inputs to the children at the click of a button. These kids strutted around masquerading as the '*know alls*', while leaving in their wake, a dejected lot with a massive IQ complex.

At home for parents, it was like fighting an unknown and unseen rival who somehow enjoyed greater credibility than us. Somehow this new guru on the internet had an undefinably greater power in satisfying the millennials' curiosity and earning their intellectual loyalty. By the time the new millennium dawned, most of us parents had slowly and steadily started succumbing to the omniscient power of the internet.

Pronto! answers were available on the internet and the millennials could steal a march over their mates because information is power, right? A kid who had all the answers was almost always held in high esteem. Well, at least in the eyes of those who were still without the device and the connection. The silent internet guru was also making millennials important for teachers, parents, grandparents, and complete strangers on the streets because they were the ones with information almost in real time. They could find picnic places, great dine outs, addresses and locations, and book tickets for movies and live shows. They were the go-to persons and they could feel the power that they were wielding over others, having become 'experts' on practically everything. Kids were caught in an idea that – their parents and elders appeared to know less, while they knew more, and faster.

In many households Google had taken centerstage and had started being held in high esteem. All of a sudden, I found myself in competition and to my ignominy not with the school teacher or contemporary mothers, or even the neighbor's Mom, but yes, the neighbor's kids!

I found that almost all parents had these newfound rivals to deal with — kids who possessed personal phones and/or had some degree of access to the internet.

What was played out in my children's case was happening to a vast majority of contemporary moms and dads. The sea change in the manner in which the kids were being raised and receiving their early education played out in many different ways in the years to come. The interesting part here is that what was being experienced at that time made limited sense when the events were actually taking place. Everything was changing, children's lives, their parents and families, the teaching and learning environment in schools, and the whole macrocosm to which the millennial kids of that time were exposed.

The generation unwittingly tuned into the big, wide (virtual) world via the internet was less likely to accept the parents' and teachers' word as the final word.

To my further chagrin, it was in this very period of dwindling respect for teachers that I had decided to embark on an academic career.

TEACHING MILLENNIALS

Having joined the world of teaching around the turn of the century, little did I know that it was going to be millennial kids that I was going to teach as a university professor.

While I had grown up in the *analog* world, the kids sitting before me were raised in the *digital* world. Adolescents around me, glued as they were to their screens, were absorbing information from all over and of all kinds. In Asia, the few years before the millennium, were defining years.

I noticed and recall vividly that early attempts at virtual experimentation meant coming up with identities for emails. This was essential to connect to the world wide web. Whether young or old, you needed to create your own identity and send it out there into the void. At that time, kids ran amuck rechristening themselves differently from what their parents had so proudly bestowed upon them as their birth names. They were willing to shed their given birth identities and choose exotic ones like *sugarsweetme@.....* or *iamdabest@......*

These exotica however co-existed with staid ones. To earlier generations it would not so much as occur to change their identities, even if it meant 'waiting in a queue' for it to be allotted. It was a natural thing for them to retain their names, for example *monashah2001@....* or *johnmills99@......* Looking back, I chuckle when I think of how the older generation willingly queued up to receive the 99th position, without so much as a murmur, despite being pipped by the very first John Mills who got to the virtual hustings much earlier, claiming the top spot as *johnmills01@.....!* They seemed to be content in retaining their birth name, perhaps even grateful that the internet was kind enough not take it away from them! Why grateful? Maybe because the virtual identity came for 'free' and with very few strings attached. This illustration subtly points to the vast differences in the way the two generations indulged in self-expression.

Millennial kids used it as a means of self-evocation, happy to break free from impositions, into a world of their own while the older generations clung to their identities. They were exercising the new found freedom of choice bestowed by the internet messiah. Gone were the shackles of everyday parental dos and don'ts. The Internet was their refuge, their very own hiding place as it were. Trading their birth names for more fanciful ones is only one example of how they were on their way to discovering themselves, *all by themselves.* In short, the *analog* generation of parents was giving way to their *digital* progeny, with significant repercussions.

The *digital* progeny – the millennials discovered a world apart and away from fairy tales and classics. They found themselves in a world which did not grow on them steadily, but which kind of exploded all around them. With information on their fingertips, their lives changed overnight. Entertainment, reading, access to publications, and planning meetings both regular and clandestine became that much easier. Being in constant touch with friends across the world became easy, so who needed picnics and family quality time?

I landed in a milieu quite different from the one in which I had been raised. I wasn't exactly thrilled to face an invisible competitor in the room. When it came to kids, this competitor was wily and had decided to take the fight right into our homes. In the classrooms, at work, and at home, teaching and learning had acquired a whole new dimension.

A teacher or parent as the bearer of knowledge and books as the repository of knowledge were swiftly becoming at least partially redundant. A parent or teacher was no longer the first line of inquiry. It was either friends or the internet. Dissecting discussions on the teacher's teaching prowess and knowledge levels were carried out through chats and messenger apps, with google playing the information intermediary.

CHANGED LEARNING LANDSCAPE BEFORE AND AFTER THE 1980S

By the early years of the new millennium, a lot many things changed. Once the only way for college going students to express themselves was by indulging in either sports or signing up for hobby and culture clubs. Club memberships dwindled ironically when college enrolments in India actually increased exponentially. Most of the campuses wore a deserted look soon after classes where decades earlier one would have witnessed friendly banter and carefree chatter in small or large groups. A typical college cafeteria in our times was either abuzz with heated discussions or in holy communion with the food. I started seeing youth sitting around tables with food, yet hardly in conversation with each other. The conversations were happening through chats on phones with persons across the table or with significant others located elsewhere!

The learning landscape too underwent a sea change. Careful immersion in books and publications was replaced by unimaginative stuffing of information with little or no scope for reflection. While raising millennials, we experienced closely the growing emphasis and competition to score better grades to the point of leading many children to emotional and mental distress even before they had completed high school. As kids, instead of developing a love for life-long learning, a majority of the millennials deep down, were cynical towards education.

When dealing with college students on a day-to-day basis, I found tendencies in a large number of them to go through their learning, seeking quick fixes and easy solutions. In the same period, one of my own millennial kid was in college. He found college to be the worst period of his life. The way in which learning was happening in the classrooms had left the millennials bereft of their love for learning. Most times they were unwilling to accept the boring, and often listless methods of teaching by the faculty. The same opinion was echoed by most of the students who were receiving their degrees from middling or premier institutions around the country. This prevailing feeling cut across all types of education.

I admit, I was hardly prepared for the vastly altered classroom. I could not identify with these new beings seated in front of me. Earlier, as merely an occasional lecturer in B-schools, I had failed to see the imperceptible changes that had crept into the classroom. By the new millennium, classrooms had undergone makeovers, with most of the B-schools becoming equipped with broadband and other amenities. Gone were the virtues of frugality and simplicity of the past. The classrooms that I entered were spruced up, well-equipped, modern, and student-friendly. As I stepped into these portals little did I know how much my life would change.

Firstly, tuition fee was being revised very frequently as it was necessary to attract good teaching talent. Inflationary trends did not help much to keep the costs within reasonable limits either; material, equipment, and human costs were steadily on the rise. Access to world-class data for research was another challenge but was necessary for encouraging research and learning activities in the institutions.

Secondly, students and households too had undergone a sea change. Changing demographic trends pointed to a higher socioeconomically aspirant class of people seeking the very best returns on their investment in education. Parents as major stakeholders and influencers in the choice of education were demanding more from their investments.

On their part, students had the access to information to compare where the best, optimum, or worst offers were available. And what do you think they referred to the most, after parents and a close circle of well-wishers? Well their peers, of course. Peers who were not necessarily from their immediate circle of friends but the wider, open, vast universe made accessible through the internet. In other words, the *Quoras and Reddits* of the world.

Chatrooms and education guidance sites mushroomed with students freely interacting and dissecting academic institutions. Earlier there was no dealing with an unknown entity, distant and faceless, not always credible, and with power to ruin the reputation of an existing institution. None of us in academic management nor professors like me drawn from the industry were actually prepared for this. It was like fighting an unknown enemy.

Most of the managements were found tardy in addressing the elephant in the room because they were clueless about how to deal with it. Any academic institution builds its reputation incrementally, its faculty and alumni add to the reputation over long years. Like wine, the older the institution, the better acknowledged it is. People in various walks of their professional lives, in flesh and blood grow its name, adding to its fame.

How then could our mindsets shaped over centuries accept the virtual dissections of real depth of knowledge and the ethos of an institution? Blind reverence and deep gratitude, as I mentioned earlier, was the only way we had learnt to think of our alma maters. Deep reverence is what we held in our hearts for the professors and the portals. The mind was outraged and shocked when the internet threw up distasteful stories.

In the classroom, students asked me strange questions. Strange, because I would never have dreamt of *demanding* answers of the administrators. It would've been frowned upon. We simply had to *know* about a college's reputation through its faculty and alumni heroes. Well I was in for a surprise, the students now needed justifications as to why institution X was better than Y. Or about the specific pedagogy that was adopted for learning and worse, what were the *guarantees* that the institution could offer, when it came to industry recruitments!

You may well dismiss these observations and even scoff at them. But, let me tell you that most of our generation considered it overstepping the boundaries. Educational institutions were hallowed temples of learning and faculty members, objects of reverence. Questioning their abilities to act as mediums of individual success was not to be. Their role was to teach the parochial and universal, after which they stepped aside. It was for the individual to prepare his or her own path of success in the world of work, making sense of all that had been learnt within these portals. One never questioned the teaching; it was always the learning.

It seemed that by the time I entered this profession, the students had morphed into being 'customers' and therefore were entitled to all explanations as deemed necessary to materialize a 'sale.' And mind you, the student, like any other customer, had to be provided an experience of a lifetime whether it was in school or college.

The university no longer meant midnight toils and lazy pursuits, it became a place of plush and plenty, with attractive ambience and lifestyle experiences. 24/7 coffee shops supplied them indulgence in fast food, well-furnished rooms were deemed necessary for inducing prep study, and well-designed and well-equipped places to 'hang out' were necessary for entertaining and recreation.

The repercussions of the infotech revolution and the internet and the newfound perceptions of education changed irrevocably. Before we could say '*jack robinson*' time-tested teaching techniques also had to undergo a change. Poring over long and laborious tomes went out of the window, plodding through seemingly unintelligible language gave way to simple and easy to comprehend approaches, with less verbose text.

Millennials felt a certain impatience with all things slow, immersive, and laborious. Immersion and assimilation were no longer in vogue as a learning prerequisite by the millennial cohort. Learning preferences were more parochial than universal. Education had to be modular, and 'fit for the purpose.' The attitude towards learning was limited to the direct benefits in relation to getting employment or solving an immediate problem. Expansive and visionary inputs forcing the student to mull in depth, were increasingly met with impatience. This phenomenon was gripping not only the STEM faculties but also the traditionally free -wheeling humanities and liberal arts.

The time-tested 'quest and self-discovery' that came with visiting the libraries and sitting in holy communion among the books, gave way to google and mastering of concepts through 'one minute' bullet-pointed dispensations. Education took on a completely different hue. This was expected in the changed scenario and the teacher had no choice but to stay relevant by falling in line with the change.

For diehard traditionalists this meant digging in their feet and resisting the change. As for my kind, it meant accepting the change, albeit selectively. I started thinking of ways of not throwing away the best of instruction that our generation had received and its accompanying joy of learning. This also meant that I had to learn the ways of the *Digitals*, sooner than later to be 'accepted' as one of their own. It meant establishing a relationship with them and coming across as someone 'cool.' Yes, it did mean constant innovations in pedagogic delivery by 'listening' to the bunch of adults before me.

All was not well in the early days. My early teaching days dealt me some good and some nasty cards and unexpected surprises. In the intervening years, the world had changed and I found myself right in the vortex of that change. As the days progressed, I found myself frequently seeking the company of veteran educators in the household partly to seek affirmation of what still held good when it came to education. Soon, I started figuring out the terminal values of education, those that could never be compromised regardless of generation. In this I was greatly influenced by the philosophy of the *gurukul*[9] *system practiced in ancient India and Kahlil Gibran's*[10] *beautiful evocation of what a teacher must be.* The lines that influenced me the most were

"If he is indeed wise, he does not bid you enter the house of his wisdom, But rather leads you to the threshold of your own mind"

For instance, I started carefully and consciously crafting a style that was not going to compromise the quality of teaching-learning, while accommodating the internet in it. I was never in doubt that the kind of image that I painstakingly built in the minds of my student stakeholders would be of a person balanced between the past, the contemporary, and the future.

I mentally shrugged off the thought of remaining in their collective memory as an inconsequential and beleaguered relic. If anything, I had to first live up to my parents' unparalleled reputation before I went ahead and created my own. So, for now between the home and the world, I was the professor in transition. A transition with so many dimensions.

For me the world had changed inexorably and how!

---

9 A gurukul is a traditional school in India with students (shishya) living near their guru, often in the same dwelling, as a sort of family. Before the British rule, the gurukuls were South Asia's main form of education. www.yogapedia.com/definition/5439/gurukul

10 Kahlil Gibran was a nineteenth century poet and artist who wrote The Prophet. https://poets.org/poem/teaching

CHAPTER 3

Millennials from the Eyes of Gen Xers/Baby Boomers

With little time to spare in the early days of being a full time academic and administrator, 'SMS' was the go-to medium to keep up with family and close friends. Before I knew it, SMS was passé and I had to move to WhatsApp. I drew the line with WhatsApp. Social media like Facebook, Twitter, Instagram, LinkedIn, and Snapchat were nothing more than words for me. Though for me this virtual world rested in the strange and unknown, I attempted to keep up with the phenomenon that was engulfing the world by reading articles and asking my homegrown millennials about it.

I thought I needed to keep up at least intellectually, to know more about this beast called social media to help me 'deal' with it. I read articles of its effects and effectiveness, and its power to influence through connecting and networking. I followed its use, misuse, and abuse by people scrupulously. I read and heard innumerable arguments in favor and against it from several quarters. Soon I realized that a decade into this century the world was divided on one more premise — those who had access to social media and those who did not.

I found myself in a miniscule minority of those Gen Xers/Baby Boomers like me, who had access, but *chose* not be part of this world.

Of course, like me, this miniscule ilk faced innumerable taunts and slights for being 'backward thinking.' In the meanwhile, smart phones had added humongous torque to this tsunami. In 2020, there were reportedly 3.9 billion global users of social networking sites (Datareportal).[11]

---

[11] Social Media Users. https://datareportal.com/social-media-users

There were any number of advocates of social networking, extolling the virtues of connecting with long-lost friends, mates and even remote celebrities, who came ever so close almost overnight. It gave them a window into an expanded world, watching intimate details of their lives unfolding in real time. They could make or break celebrities, icons, and change-makers with a quick thumbs up or thumbs down on a social media site.

A movie painstakingly made, a book long labored over, a government policy deliberated and thoughtfully proposed, were either dismissed or appreciated with apparently no logical analysis. Gone were the days of intense discussions and lively debates. For someone of my generation this scheme of things appeared arbitrary and fraught with danger. It was driven by emotions rather than analyses. The thumbs up or down was iconic of an age that signified strongly the posit of '*I Matter*'. The unintended consequences of '*I Matter*' was that the wisdom of the earlier generation faced a danger of simply evaporating… *pooff*…in the face of a thumbs down.

For one, almost everybody began to crave for this power to make or break the existing status quo. You can well imagine how this power must have affected the youth who were the prime consumers of the internet and the social networking world. Millennials came to wield a lot of power, the power of not only information but also the power of being proximate to any change that occurred around them in real time. They were constantly connected and that made all the difference.

I decided to get myself in line with the ways of the world. Uninitiated as I was, Alisia Grover, a millennial colleague in 2016, advised and directed me to LinkedIn, a 'serious' site for professionals. I would need to create a 'profile' to get the maximum benefits of the algorithm that matched my profile with others with similar searches. After considerable effort and many faux pas' while signing up, I now have a page built entirely as the site has prescribed; this page is rated as '*All Star*.' I had a sense of private gratification that an algorithm found me worthy of being a star! Needless to say, to get the stars I had to fill out each and every line in the form, even when my mind wasn't too convinced, I needed to tick all the boxes.

If I felt like dropping some detail, a prompt appeared informing me of the consequence. I recall not being too happy 'to be told' by an invisible, seemingly imperious entity what was best for me. When I shared this with my kids and a few of my students, they simply shrugged it off. The shrug signified, *Hey- isn't- that- obvious -what's- the- big -deal*? I particularly recall the section on 'Volunteering' that I hesitated filling up. We had always been taught to be generous and reach out to people in need, however, it had to be done anonymously and straight from the heart. I struggled to write the charities with which I was associated. Finally, I decided to include a youth volunteer organization, which I felt matched with the algorithm's needs and my comfort with non-disclosure.

The next advice from the sage and savvy in social media was to initiate my identity on Facebook. The habitual laggard in the social networking adoption cycle was about to get another identity in this fast-populating cyber world. It was gratifying to see that within a month of joining I had notched up friend requests from 1,400 people and had added a further 997 to my list. Of those who are connected with me on Facebook and LinkedIn, the overwhelming majority are millennials as they are the student cohorts I have taught at the university.

I may be reading something more into this, but it seems to me that the flood of friend requests was an indication of telling this 'stodgy' old woman to buck up. It was as though they were lending me a hand and hauling me on to the social media parapet. It also felt that they were enthusiastic about remaining connected with their professor. This seemed very familiar and old school, similar to the emotional connect we had with our erstwhile professors.

Imagine how this must be playing out for the millions of millennials on Facebook and LinkedIn, a zillion times over, 24/7, when someone, somewhere was constantly acknowledging you. Coming back to the implications of the thumbs up or down mentioned earlier from somebody not in person before me, help me understand its genuineness?

Detractors may argue that even in person, there is, of course, no fool proof way of knowing whether the acknowledgement is genuine. However, as Generation Xers we had been schooled in the time- tested adages *seeing is believing, never judge a book by its cover,* and *the proof of the pudding is in the eating*. Call me what you may, to this day I am truly puzzled about the sincerity of a thumbs up or a thumbs down, as a fool proof determinant of having done something good (or not so good) in the eyes of others.

However, once in the vortex, there is no way to stop the pronounced verdicts that appear throughout the day, week, and year. For every new posting that was uploaded there appeared a Newtonian 'equal and opposite reaction'. I realized that this phenomenon which fascinated me, was something the millennials have lived with for decades now. It was in this yo-yo world of instant feedback that they grew up. If a 'like or not like' could affect the older and perhaps a more emotionally resilient generation, I can only imagine what it must have done to the young millennial users of social networking sites. So wrapped up were they in this world of the virtual that more often than not, the real must have seemed unreal to them. Did this constant badger of likes and not likes unobtrusively shape their psyche as they grew up?

My social media sojourn began only after my full-time position in academia ended. I served in several highly reputed educational institutions in the western and northern part of India like the Symbiosis Institute of International Business (SIIB), The National Institute of Construction Management and Research (NICMAR) in Pune, and the RICS School of Built Environment- Amity University, Delhi NCR[12]. Through continuous research and acquisition of academic accolades, in a moment of epiphany I voluntarily decided to retire from active service to pursue my other life goals. Moving away from a stable place where ex-students came and visited me when I moved on, left many searching for me. Some moved out of India too into faraway lands. This compelled me to open a Facebook account and then a Twitter and Instagram!

Almost overnight from a detached, secluded microcosm I have got caught in the vortex of my students' fast paced life and I am able to witness their personal capers via FB and their professional progress through LinkedIn.

I have realized that the simple algorithm I gauged in my first-hand experience is that social media's power of multiplication is behind its power of amplification.

GEN X/BABY BOOMERS AND THE MILLENNIALS

It all started with my daily rendezvous with millennials at work while also raising two others at home. I started noticing clear distinctions between

---

[12] Royal Institution of Chartered Surveyors. Established 1868, in London.

them in contrast to us, the Gen Xers/Baby Boomers. More of these contrasts between the two generations were drawn out further with every incoming cohort of students on one end and the Gen X /Baby Boomer faculty group at the university on the other.

I spent considerable time with both groups in various capacities and so was a close witness to the way they thought and acted. For students, as their professor, mentor, guide, dean, program in-charge, go-to person, and *'away parent,'* there emerged patterns of behavior that enabled me to draw a few conclusions about the behavioral, intellectual, and emotional characteristics of the millennials. These characteristics were obvious consequences of the upbringing that most of them had been subjected to.

For those born in Generation X there are significant differences in the way we spent our times vis-a-vis the millennials. There are sceptics who consider the millennial generation as one which feels it is entitled to receive concessions or expected to be bullish about what they ought to possess simply by virtue of being born into this world. In other words, they appear to 'expect' their parents and society to make things available to them even if they come across to others as those who don't 'deserve' the advantages.

Baby Boomers/Gen X had been raised by their parents in relative affluence too. Even so, the values drilled into them lay somewhere in the realm of *there's no such thing as a free lunch* or *if anything significant has to be achieved in one's life, one has to burn the midnight oil.* These oft repeated statements worked their way into the deepest psyche of Baby Boomers/Gen X. Little wonder then, as their professors the millennials' relative nonchalance, flippancy, sneers, and attitudes, frustrated many.

In this conundrum that faced us, I found myself wanting to know more about them, how their minds worked, and what their emotions were made of. This curiosity enabled me to procrastinate a little more when it came to slotting them into black or white, right or wrong, focused or distracted, selfish or altruistic. The protracted time at the university further enabled me to develop a strong bond with millennial students.

Like all human cohorts, millennials too have gone through the typical phases of life -- infanthood, childhood, adolescence, and adulthood. As with all generations earlier, millennials were deeply influenced by the generation closest to them, in this case, the Baby Boomers/ Gen X. Despite this there was a vast difference between the millennial generation and its predecessors, when it came to the individuality of the millennials. If one were to ask millennials about whose influences were the strongest in shaping their personalities there will be the usual suspects viz. parents, teachers, friends, celebrities, and reference groups. However, what is interesting to know is the changed *intensity* of these influences.

Along with the usual ones mentioned earlier, technology emerged as the greatest influencer in shaping millennial mindsets. Mind you, not just any technology, but *information technology* (IT). Seen from the Baby Boomer/ Gen X's perspective, IT literally burst onto the whole planet changing the way we lived and worked. When it came to millennials though, it gained the most traction and became a way of life. For millennials, embedding of IT in their lives is the single most intensive influence, perhaps next only to their parents. IT spread through devices like PCs, laptops, or mobiles, and was so insidious that it *paled all other influencers* in comparison.

It is not surprising that using technology for understanding the world has affected the way millennials perceive the world. Information technology enabled millennials to stay connected 24/7. For instance, the adolescent Gen Xers had found friends using the classic clique method, *you- are- in- my- clique- so- we- filter- and-keep- out- all-others.* This way of adding friends back then resulted in millions of Gen Xers facing childhood loneliness. They were likely victims of spiteful classmates who might have classified them as 'weird' simply because they were not from a particular social class or were being raised by a single parent. With the advent of social networking sites, all this changed and millennials could be what they wished to be and reach out and add 'friends' from across the world.

Life was not so lonely and wretched if one was accepted in a community, based on what persona was projected.

CHARACTERISTICS OF GEN XERS

Millennials were born to parents from Baby Boomers/ Gen X who themselves had been given a slightly more affluent life relative to their parents, across all income cohorts. For example, a Gen Xer born even in a working-class family enjoyed a far better standard of living that came from an improved purchasing power. Labor rights were given prime importance by the governments of the time, higher levels of education and skill development resulted in rising employment with the Silent Generation/ Baby Boomers doing economically better. Many of the innovations that had emanated from the Apollo space missions were available to consumers due to the patents being advanced to manufacturers for commercial production. Some of these were the microwaves, the ball point pens, poly fabric, and breathing devices. These when made available to people had led to the subsequent generations vastly benefit from their use. Goods were cheap due to the economies of scale of large- scale production and a variety of options were available suited to different socioeconomic segments. There was an increase in general affluence in the western world and some Asian countries.

The phrase *Customer Is King* coined by management guru Peter Drucker and *The Customer is Always Right* by leading retailers Gordon of Selfridges, and other retailers like Wanamaker and Marshall Field, enabled Gen Xers to buy at prices suitable for their pockets. Gen X was the first of the generations after World War II to witness the consumer revolution. It was the generation at whom intensive marketing was targeted aka *the Buy One Get One Free* nudges or the highly differentiated products that multiplied consumers' choice options.

Gen X was the first generation to be educated about the differences in beauty products, personalized products, apparel, and even food. For the first time, hand me downs and frugality went out of the window in favor of indulgence and feel good mantras. A household in the 1950s shared a cake of soap, Gen Xers had personalized soaps reflecting the individual needs based on gender (male/female), stage of life (infant/school going/ teenager), type of skin (oily/dry), purpose (beauty/medicated/freshness), and all permutations and combinations therein. Breakfast cereal too underwent a sea change in its traditional promise of providing a simple, wholesome meal to start a busy day. All of a sudden, the humble cereal convinced the Gen X mom that it had metamorphosed into an elixir that was important as it provided vitality to the brain!

With baseline prosperity available to the majority, Gen X resembled the Silent Generation in its attitudes. Its members were hugely individualistic, wanted to 'earn' their way to affluence, were exposed to new ideas and independent thought, and were also realistic. In short, they believed in bringing about change through their efforts, rather than waiting for things to materialize on their own.

By and large, Gen Xers knew the importance of education and were willing to take the pains to continue learning despite having jobs and starting families. This is borne out well by the fact that Gen Xers did not always seek out comfortable government jobs or corporate jobs despite a whole lot of them pursuing qualifications suitable for those. In my own B-school class of 1987, only 30 percent ended up working for corporates. All others went the entrepreneurial way at different points in time in their professional careers. Most of the cohort wanted to chart its own territory. Little wonder then that the highest number of start-up founders in the US (55 percent), are from Generation X.[13] Gen Xers exhibited values like individualism and realism. Their individualism also made them competitive.

Gen X typified the nuclear family type, largely urbanized and earning double incomes, with delayed child bearing as the predominant characteristics. Within the Gen X emerged segments based on their incomes, occupations, and educational backgrounds. The terms Yuppies, Dinks, Dewks, Mobys and Koopfs were popular acronyms used for describing them.[14]

Gen Xers were conscious of providing and passing on the benefits of their higher living standards to their children. The younger Gen X members were known as Yuppies who had typical characteristics, were professionals with large salary packages, and were exposed to intense competition at the workplace.

Being individualistic and upwardly mobile, they bought goods and services that were aspirational. Their choices veered towards branded products and those which promised exclusivity. They bought exotic properties in suburbia, drove swanky cars, opted for luxury vacations, and had either no kids or very few. Gen Xers had contraceptives to keep family numbers low and disposable incomes high. To the class of Yuppies belonged the '*aspirationals*' who though not in fast paced jobs were equally in a hurry to change their fortunes through hard work,

---

13 Anna Sofia Martin, 2016. The Undetected Influence Of Generation X. See: https://www.forbes.com/sites/nextavenue/2016/09/13/the-undetected-influence-of-generation-x/#fd814491efbd

14 Yuppies– Young Upwardly Mobile Professionals; Dinks– Double Income No Kids; Dewks– Double Earners With Kids; Mobys– Mother Older, Baby Younger; Koopfs- Kids Of One Parent Families.

continuous learning, and grit. Gen X was more willing to either forgo parenthood or at least delay it to ensure that their wards got the very best of the material world. Typically, these sections of Gen X evolved into being called Dinks or Dewks. The millennials were born to Yuppy parents. Typical Yuppy homes had all the time saving gadgets and larger houses with amenities oriented for children; creches and day cares grew and thrived in neighborhoods and annual family vacations were a must.

This was a result of more women joining the workforce and thus being able to add to the family income. For the first time in modern history, Gen X women had many more choices. Not only did they have more choices, they also had the wherewithal to exercise them. Delayed marriages, deferred child bearing, financial choices, more legal backing, women friendly work policies, better access to education and higher education in particular, and right to use contraception without religious or social censure, were some of the remarkable enablers for the women of this generation.

The growing number of Mobys among Gen Xers was a result of postponing child bearing in favor of fulfilling career aspirations and becoming financially stable with practically no social stigma. Fortuitously, the working women among this generation were more open to new ideas than women of the earlier generations.

In every other aspect, a Gen X woman had distinct traits that came with being more informed. For instance, these women tended to rely on scientific inputs than mere word of mouth information while making purchases. They were active decision makers in family matters. They were discerning customers. Choice of schools, or after-school engagements for the kids be it sports, music, additional tuitions or community engagements were scrutinized and decided by mothers.

Interestingly, Gen X women also got to decide whether they wanted to remain in marriage or not. An iconic book of the time by Avery Corman, *Kramer Vs Kramer*, depicted a woman's right to choose career over family while simultaneously depicting men as equally capable of raising a child as single parents. This book depicted the biggest departure from the traditional and popular belief of 'a happy family is a family which has both parents, with the mother as the strongest pivot.'

More millennials were witness to divorces and single parent homes than the earlier generations.

Gen X had a high degree of exposure to technology as it became the first generation to use computing devices outside the workplace. Desk top computers with printers (DTPs), brought computers into households and took a pride of place in the study and library space of most suburban homes, family rooms, or even on kitchen boards for quick access to housewives. They became an indispensable item in American households in the 1980s and early 1990s. Michael Dell, himself a Gen Xer, led Dell Inc to become a *Fortune 500* company by selling customized PCs to the Gen X, Yuppy, Dinks and Dewk families, the world over.

In short Gen X was an *avantgarde* and trend setting generation which was technologically savvy.

GEN X VERSUS MILLENNIALS: A STUDY IN CONTRAST

How many Gen Xers can recall their childhood and adolescent years? How different were those days from the ones that the millennials went through? A peek down memory lane offers colorful insights of Gen Xers blundering through those years. One of the prominent themes for Gen Xers was the school proms and annual college fests. In fact, such events were cause for putting up dramatic emotions on display. Moving on from old friendships, rivalries, crushes, heartbreaks were grist for many a potboiler. Youth based events provided an easy backdrop pitting rival teams against established cliques cheering or booing each other.

Many will recall that growing up, Gen X members recorded their mush feelings for each other rather painstakingly with the help of yearbooks or slam books. These books were generally pocket sized in which 'the chosen ones' had to handwrite meaningful quotes to be preserved as keepsakes. Sounds quite silly and archaic to the millennials, who have no use for a slam book, when they can Facebook instead.

In fact, the Gen Xers held diametrically opposite views about music, dating, and hanging out. For Gen Xers the ultimate sense of advantage was buying Beatles and country music albums on Long Play (LP) records, attending Woodstock to listen to the likes of Jimi Hendrix or head out to Newport for Bob Dylan. Rolling Stones, Frank Zappa, Janice Joplin, and the very famous Indian sitarist Ravi Shankar were sublime heroes. For Gen Xers such music filled their souls and beckoned them to follow a counterculture (the Hippie culture). Their unswerving loyalty to their bands ensured that their favorite bands remained on the top of the charts for weeks and months at a time. With the millennials, all things slow and savory were thrown out. In came a 13-year-old Canadian, Justin Bieber in 2007, who smashed all records in a single week. This bopper was no exception and had only joined the club of millennials led by Britney Spears, Miley Cyrus, and Demi Lovato. Getting to the top of the charts was not a matter of a year, but a mere week or two and remaining there did not seem to be much priority.

How many of the Gen X's members will swear to having reached their current positions in life by toiling in the school library, poring over tomes, and scribbling notes while Gen Y finds it ridiculous to spend valuable hours in a lonely and friendless place surrounded by books? For millennials fingertip access to information was sorted, with the advent of internet and e-libraries.

In the case of Gen Xers, the coming of age sagas were portrayed through movies like the *Dead Poets Society*, *American Graffiti*, and *the Breakfast Club*. While the millennials lapped up the transition from childhood to adolescence through *Super Bad* or *The Sisterhood of the Travelling Pants* and the most popular television series the *Friends*!

When it came to a 'voice' in family matters there was a world of difference between the generations. Unlike Gen Xers whose parents were relatively more hierarchical, millennials had a great deal of voice in their families. They were an obviously more indulged generation, as many Gen X parents experienced financial upswings that accompanied rising career graphs.

Being someone who works in the domain of built environment, it piques me to know how different generations interact with space. I find there is an interesting way in which millennials interact with spaces. For instance, for Gen Xers, as malls mushroomed in cities and they turned parents, they got used to treating these places as a means to get several activities done under one roof with the family. It was normal to have young urban families spending entire days on weekends at malls with their Moms buying household goods, while the Dads minded the kids in the play area. It was planned as a family outing with meals and movies completing the day. Kids were given choices of which places to enter, which toys to buy or choose colors of their liking.

In contrast have you seen the millennials maneuvering the malls? Do you think their primary motive is to shop? Well think again. If you look closely you will find that most millennials are languidly browsing through the stores. The bulk of them are found at Starbucks or hanging out waiting for their group of friends in open food courts or at gaming stations. Malls for millennials are hang out spaces. So where did you think they buy their clothes?

Online of course!

It was common to find millennials participating in major buying decisions in families. They were consulted and invited to offer their choices of brands, or holiday destinations for family vacations. Many even helped by supplying the relevant background information based on surfing and peer group recommendations. Being on their own at home gave them a high degree of freedom of choice accompanied by solitude. Supervision was mostly by remote parents who were at work. Even kids' moms at home were able to grab more autonomy when it came to choosing clothes, tuitions, and pocket money. All in all, across all income segments, millennials enjoyed far more freedom of choice than the earlier generations. Mobile telephony, the internet, and increased economic mobility of their parents added to the self-assurance of this generation.

One of the consequences of their affinity to technology resulted in the Gen Xers providing their children (the millennials) with personal phones. Perhaps they had selfish motives for doing this. For instance, parents felt that they would be able to track their kids' whereabouts and activities in real time using their personal phones. That was about all. Never in their wildest dreams would they have known the life changing effect this gadget would have on the whole generation.

What the phone did to the millennials was phenomenal. It ended up influencing an entire generation of children who were the first to lap up all the exciting possibilities of the device irreversibly so. This midget of a gadget with the internet within, held the millennial generation in thrall. All chimeras of the earlier kinds that Gen X held dearly as its own, gave way to the Netscapes, AltaVistas, and WebCrawlers of the world even before Google became the preferred master.

Almost overnight fairy tales, phantom tales, Spider Man, Batman, Superman, Axa, and the quintessential Barbie doll, so dear to Gen X in their growing up years, were discarded by their kids. What found favor with the millennials were the GI Joes, Ninja Turtles, Playstations, Cabbage Patch Kids, Pokemons, and Aibos.

Electronics had hit the toy and games scene big time.

MILLENNIALS, TECHNOLOGY, AND GEN XERS

The millennial generation was the first to be born into a wired world. While smartphones are now common across all age groups, their biggest users are among the millennials. Compared to Gen X, millennials consumed technology in a different way. For one, they were not afraid of trying out new things, could communicate easily with machines, and perhaps even considered machines as extensions of themselves.

Let me share with you the case of my own household millennials and their interactions with all things non-tech.

Like any parent would, I dutifully took it upon myself to teach my young kids basic banking or post office transactions. Back then, neighborhood post offices did exist, situated round the corner, for those were still the days of hand written letters, and dispatching parcels by sticking loads of postage stamps. Therefore, one needed to visit the post office to purchase stamps or other postage material. Bank outlets were also available in close by areas. As school going kids, I would send them to run errands.

I felt and I may be completely biased about this but the kids took a lifetime to learn simple transactions of filling out money withdrawal forms or cashing or depositing a cheque. There was always a huge delay returning home. Willy-nilly, I found myself gently castigating them while extolling our smartness in learning 'important' transactions flawlessly. However, they were not ones to be subdued, and always countered my arguments. They found the process downright tedious and loathed dealing with lackadaisical and unfriendly folks behind the counters. Predictably so, the argument was never solved, there was only more petulance on their part and irritation on mine. The whole scenario changed when Automatic Teller Machines arrived on the scene and emails replaced hand written letters with postage stamps. Peace reigned as the kids happily transacted with ATMs and we started sending our letters through emails.

In another incident I distinctly recall a housewarming celebration, when we moved into a new house which was also planned as a family reunion involving many family members. It meant buying large amounts of stuff. I decided to enlist the help of my two robust teenager sons to choose and also carry the parcels through crowded and narrow inner streets of the city. Well what for me was an exciting afternoon, having got the best bargains from the shop owners, didn't quite match my kids' sentiments. We had barely put down the tons of stuff in the kitchen, when all hell broke loose. The earful that I received from them, is etched in my memory to this day.

The moot point of their rebellion was their disgust at being in crowded, cramped places, carrying tons of stuff through the heat and grime. They were angry and frustrated with my idea of spending the afternoon this way and tagging them along. They vowed and warned me that not only was this an unnecessary exercise but that I should never ever indulge in it again. By now, you too must think the boys were uncaring and cavalier.

Imagine my chagrin when I learnt that they had found my smartness rather misplaced. They sat me down, flipped open the online shopping sites and showed me the even larger discounts I had missed out on. They pointed out to me that instead of the unwarranted effort of negotiating crabby shopkeepers, narrow by-lanes, and traffic snarls, online was way smarter even for the pocket. At that time shopping online for me was like traversing an unknown path, fraught with dangers that come with the absence of the 'touch, feel, and smell' of traditional shopping. The millennials had taken to it as the smartest way to get what they wanted.

While the older generation quaked at the sight of new software and applications, the millennials took to it like fish to water. This of course, is an advantage in the workplace where rapidly changing technology drives business success.

As you see, this was a different generation in the making, which I could not have recognized back then.

CHAPTER 4

Decoding the Millennial Psyche, the Gen X Way

TECH IS THEIR PET

One of the most prominent factors that distinguish the millennials from Gen X is their massive familiarity with and the use of technology. They adored gadgets as they would their pets! In the US, 83 percent of the millennials reported sleeping with their smart phones. On the opposite side of the world, in Australia, a Deloitte Mobile Consumer Survey found that 18- to 24-year-olds checked their phones up to 56 times a day and some checked it more than 200 times daily.[15] Another survey of 2,000 Australians using a wider sample of participants aged between 18-75 years revealed that more than 80 percent of the Australians could not last an hour after waking, before checking their phones.[16] And half of the 18- to 24-year-olds checked their phones within 5 minutes of waking.

Millennials were perpetually on call and always just a message away. I am reminded of the famous byline of a global banking giant *The Citi Never Sleeps.* Replace Citi with Millennial and you'll get what I mean. The unusual facility that my young kids had in all things tech, did not strike me as much as when I noticed the senior millennial cohorts at the university and their facile use of tech too.

---

[15] Global Mobile Consumer Survey: US Edition: A new era in mobile continues (2018). See: https://www2.deloitte.com/content/dam/Deloitte/us/Documents/technology-media-telecommunications/us-tmt-global-mobile-consumer-survey-exec-summary-2018.pdf

[16] Deloitte. Mobile Consumer Survey: The Australian Cut. (2017). See: https://www.researchgate.net/deref/https%3A%2F%2Fwww2.deloitte.com%2Fau%2Fmobile-consumer-survey

It never failed to surprise me how quickly my students in the first decade of the millennium analyzed huge data that we collected in the course of dissertation work. The secret lay in their dexterity to learn online. They could teach themselves statistical and mathematical computations using search engines and software and come up with rapid results. The speed was so fast, that within a couple of weeks after the data was collected one could expect the first cuts available for further analysis. This was a far cry from my days at the university. We had to sit in the libraries or hang out with friends who would help us mostly manually, compute the results or at best use scientific calculators. These could take weeks and weeks to complete with no guarantee that our professor would approve the accuracy of the results.

In another related instance, a growing phenomenon among my students was the hesitation and reluctance to go forth and meet people when doing their dissertation related research. A dissertation is an essential element for students who are enrolled in master's programs. In every university, this is a project driven by the students and supervised by faculty. Most times we professors preferred adding 'primary' data gathering techniques *(for e.g. personal interview technique),* which required collecting data from human respondents by meeting them and receiving their feedback. These are important for maintaining a robust firmament of the research design and have great value in producing quality research. No big deal one might say, yet I was confounded with this reluctance.

I must admit that initially I found it annoying when students placed questionnaires on Survey Monkey or Google Forms and waited for responses. As researchers, it was ingrained in us to be chary of open systems that were susceptible to hacking and compromising privacy. Another practical limitation was that we were completely dependent on the respondents when it came to filling out the forms, which led to delays in collecting the required data. Even for a Gen Xer like me, it seemed a not so ideal practice and waste of precious time. My students, however, always had a different viewpoint. They were loath to 'knock on doors', or stop strangers (however politely) on roadsides or in malls and urge them to fill out the forms. They genuinely found it a waste of time and a frivolous exercise insisted upon by a 'mad' professor. Agreed, it didn't help much when the folks were irritable, uncooperative, or downright abusive. Students were smarted and felt hurt.

As their teacher, I had to make them understand that researchers had to be 'neutral' and not take such random acts personally. I was compelled to engage in several rounds of negotiations which also involved lessons in emotional intelligence. I had to convince them that it was the hallmark of a good researcher. Negotiations also entailed convincing them of the hazards of indiscriminate dependence on a virtual platform as this could potentially wreak havoc with the eventual quality of work. One major reason was the credibility of the source of the data. And the other was the hazard of completely leaving out a tech challenged target, which could possibly throw a spanner in the whole exercise of reaching out to the target sample units. After active negotiations and convincing, they went ahead with data collection. On a good day, I would probe the reasons for their reluctance. It did turn out that they took offence at being treated rudely.

Another equally onerous reason was related to data entry. Manually entering data collected on sheets of paper into excel sheets, got to them. It was a tedious, monotonous, and useless exercise that took them away from hanging out with friends or surfing the Net. In short, far more interesting activities than doing something boring and repetitive.

Eventually we found this sweet spot of being committed to producing good quality research output, while also using the internet for adding efficiency to the process. Mercifully they came around, understanding that using technology at the cost of authenticity and reputational value was a big no. As a dissertation guide to the newer cohorts of millennials, I was not to be spared this annual 'rite of passage.'

Reflecting on those years the reasons for their apparent reluctance to meet new people could have been due to their subconscious ease with all things virtual, since childhood. The virtual became the preferred mode of establishing initial contact using social media. The first point of contact was always preferred through social media having duly *checked out* the person. Now when I write this, I realize how effortlessly millennials reached out to a complete stranger and are able to establish a connection.

Millennials like to be pre-informed about a person's professional and social profile prior to establishing contact. For old schoolers like me, sitting in the reception area of companies to meet executives and officials now seems such a waste of time and energy. But back then we were convinced by trainers and bosses that personal meetings were the most important ingredient of climbing the corporate ladder. They helped in establishing relationships, be it over a cup of tea, a game of golf, or a power luncheon. I cringe at the thought of spending hours waiting for being granted an audience ranging from a mere 2 minutes to 2 hours in my early professional career in the 1980s. We were rookies back then and thought it was our lot to be treated like this.

Not so the millennials who value their personal time more than the Gen Xers. Undoubtedly, theirs is a smarter and 'sustainable' way of reaching out and if only we could have done it their way.

To most of the Gen Xers and Baby Boomers in academia and in corporations who have been admitting millennials through their portals, the millennials came across as different. In fact, as rather indifferent and lazy. Hours were spent in faculty tea rooms, waxing eloquent on how we the Baby Boomers/Gen Xers as students were eager to learn and went out of our way to take up tough assignments. If ever there was a millennial fly on the wall in those tea rooms, I'm pretty sure it must be thinking how outdated, laborious, and pointless those efforts at learning must have been.

What one overlooked as Gen Xers was that the millennials preferred questioning existing mores and putting up resistance to all things inefficient or tedious. It was a trade - off between unnecessary labor and the time for other indulgences or pursuits.

It is perhaps only because of their constant proximity to technology that millennials automatically ended up seeking 'virtual' relief, an advantage the earlier generations lacked.

At this point it would be appropriate to mention that all things tech was not as savory as I might have given you to understand.

TECH AND THE EMOTIONAL SAPIEN

There is a darker side to technology which could endanger the mental health and well-being of millennials. I recall a sad incident that involved a bright, young girl student of mine. I write about it with a heavy heart but with the simple intent of bringing out the other side of how too much technology has the inherent potential of wreaking emotional havoc in a person's life.

Nyla was an unusually quiet young woman for a 22-year-old. Having enrolled in one of the programs and was my student. A couple of weeks into the program I found that she would be absent from the class very often. Her classmates denied any knowledge of her whereabouts. Also, she was not forthcoming in her contributions to group assignments. When it came to her individual assignments too, it was the same story. Halfway into the semester, we found her falling back in the coursework and tests. Out of concern, I enquired about her from her peers, and found that she had declined to join the others in their regular meet ups. Neither did she team up, for weekend outings with them. On those occasions when she found herself in a state of mind to attend class, she was withdrawn and unconnected, staring listlessly around her. Frequent attempts to draw her out in classroom discussions did not yield much success. At times, her absence from class continued for fairly long periods.

Fortunately, before I could take up the matter at a more serious level, she came to my office one day and poured out her tale. She had come to meet me because she felt she owed me some explanation for her behaviour. She told me that she was grateful that I was concerned about her well-being and was touched by my attempts to reach out to her quite persistently.

Nyla was a fairly good student upto her graduation in civil engineering, except in the graduating year, when her grades plunged drastically. She had been in a steady relationship with a boy a little senior to her in the same engineering college they attended. Both families knew of their bonding and were fine with the relationship. Both families thought it would be great if the two were prepared to take their relationship to its logical conclusion in the future.

The boyfriend moved to the USA to pursue a master's degree and all was fine. The relationship continued in long-distance mode thanks to WhatsApp, Skype, and similar options available at that time. It was in the last year of her graduation that the break up happened. Sadly so, virtually. Just like that! Nyla's boyfriend had found another girl in the US and decided to end his relationship with her through a cursory WhatsApp message. His Facebook pages had the new girl pinned on the wall on which he publicly professed his undying love for her.

Nyla saw this notorious display of affection and was heartbroken. When she confronted him, he blocked her on all media. She was devastated. When she reached out to her boyfriend's family, they didn't help much either. Nyla's world collapsed. She lost her mind, having invested so much in the relationship. Doctors diagnosed her state as a nervous breakdown and she was hospitalized.

When Nyla was well enough to complete her graduation exams, she could only do so after 7-8 months of therapy. The treatment was slow because of her delicate mental and emotional state. The psychiatrist prescribed drugs to enable her to maintain a mental equilibrium. After a year, her family suggested that she get back her life, and advised her to enroll in a post-graduate program to be among people of her age. This is why Nyla went through her entrance tests and enrolled in the master's program with us. However, her illness had taken its toll on her confidence. She joined the university very reluctantly. All this while she was on prescriptive drugs to avoid the suicidal thoughts that had enveloped her over the past year or so.

This explained her behavior in class, her isolation, and desire to run away from it all. The manner in which the break up happened with her boyfriend and its consequences revealed the cruel world in which the millennials lived. Never had technology appeared so ruthless to me. How could one ever be made accountable towards another human, when all that was needed was a one-sided message delivered arbitrarily to end relationships? It just did not seem fair.

After knowing her story and being grateful for sharing it with me, my efforts were directed at strengthening her, mentally and emotionally through continuous counselling. Over the next two semesters. Nyla came back to normal, improved her grades, competed for a job with her classmates, and reduced her dependency on prescriptive drugs well before she graduated. Nyla holds a good job and is serving at the executive level in a large organization. With the help of therapy and well-wishers Nyla pieced back her life leaving me to decipher why was this break up different from any other?

Breaking up and picking back the pieces in life, happens to anyone of us. With time, one learns to move on. Every person has witnessed someone else's difficult moments and perhaps even helped them overcome. At the university with so many youngsters there were bound to be numerous close encounters. Seeing Nyla go through her acute pain set me thinking about how the rejection and deep emotional wounds, debilitated a perfectly normal human being.

In the days of yore, break ups did happen but the way of communicating them ranged anywhere from a personal interface, to a note penned and left surreptitiously for the other party to read, or even the use of mutual friends who acted as couriers. The aftermath of this ranged from personal confrontation, mediation, or avoidance. These interventions took place over a period of time and somehow seemed more 'organic' as the breaking up parties had to contend with each other in the process and that too, over a period of time. Finally, when both went their ways a partial healing process was already in place. With time, one could 'heal' oneself completely.

With social media, it somehow seemed too arbitrary, one sided, and brutal. Not only was the break up one sided, it could come to anyone, as a bolt out of the blue. The insensitivity of her partner added to Nyla's pain and helplessness. Constant posting of pictures on social media only added to her grief. Frustration, indignation, and abuse are a potent combination leading to helplessness and other forms of extreme emotional distress. For me, the sobering thought was also that, like Nyla there could be many other millennials too, who must be undergoing such experiences.

Earlier generations did not have the internet in their growing up years and were therefore incapable of stalking others incessantly on social networking sites. Out of sight and physical distancing, enabled wounds to heal and helped memories fade away with time. A virtual break - up on the other hand disrespects the other person's right to appeal, the abruptness leaving no room for dialogue.

ANXIETY, STRESS, AND FEARS

Some experts hold that though millennials are known as digital natives, 58 percent have poor skills in solving emotional problems. This implies that despite being avid users of tech, they are unable to understand real life problems in social and emotional domains easily. According to psychotherapists, behavioral scientists, and researchers, millennials are an overly anxious generation.[17] They are anxious for a number of reasons. Firstly, because they fear they will not be able to maintain the same standard of living as that of their parents. Having got habituated to it, they walked into the world of work thinking their education will give them the required torque. The prolonged recession since 2008, meant this was not to be. A sizeable section of the American millennials has moved back in with their parents. Those with student loans were worse off.

To add to this, many other strange fears affect the millennials.

According to a report carried in Business Insider, in the US alone, there has been a 43 percent increase in millennials diagnosed as depressed since 2013, while another 14 percent suffered from anxiety. It was also found that they tended to seek psychotherapy more often than Gen X did, in its corresponding years[18]. According to British Heart Foundation's (BHF) *'Face a Fear'*[19] campaign, millennials are the most scared of all generations. They contend with fears arising from losing friends, spiders, bees, and wasps, saying no to social situations, phone running out of battery, of sending a text to the wrong person, missing a train or a flight, having no wi-fi, taking a photo from a bad angle, and even having their relationships destroyed. BHF is making a lot of effort to address these fears through its program and help millennials to get rid of them. These fears may sound ludicrous, funny and trivial, but think of the more

---

[17] Loren Soeiro (2019). Why Are Millennials So Anxious and Unhappy? It's not just money, dating, or finding the right job.
Blog Posted July 24. See: I Hear You. https://www.psychologytoday.com/us/blog/i-hear-you/201907/why-are-millennials-so-anxious-and-unhappy

[18] Hillary Hoffower, Allana Akhtar (2019). Lonely, burned out, and depressed: The state of millennials' mental health in 2019. OCT 10, 2019, 17:00 IST. https://www.businessinsider.in/slideshows/miscellaneous/lonely-burned-out-and-depressed-the-state-of-millennials-mental-health-in-2019/slidelist/71521961.cms#slideid=71521977

[19] Laura Nixon (2018). Fears are wreaking havoc on millennials' lives according to new research. 26 June 2018. https://www.bhf.org.uk/what-we-do/news-from-the-bhf/news-archive/2018/june/fears-are-wreaking-havoc-on-millennials-lives-according-to-new-research

profound ones that can have a debilitating effect on individuals, one of which is the *fear of failure* and its partner in crime, *the pressure of performance.*

For the millennial generation, Baby Boomers and Gen X must seem like 'Mohammed Alis' with their jaw dropping success, their astounding net worth and wealth creation, which have also added to global wealth. Naturally the millennials, though the most educated generation in history, must feel overwhelmed by their parents' stupendous success and swag. The emotional burden of keeping up and at times doing even better on ever -higher benchmarks of performance could cripple anybody, not only millennials. Sadly, unreasonable expectations begin at home, within families.

Sharing the story of Dan who went through a delicate period in his life due to an overpowering fear of failure.

> *Dan was a brilliant student in a prestigious technical university in India. His immediate family and near relations belonged to an illustrious lineage of professionals, serving bureaucrats, and industry leaders. Being admitted to the university for the bachelor's program meant competing with a million others in a nationwide competitive exam and scoring in the top 1 percentile. He enrolled in our master's program in one of the most competitive programs offered by the university.*
>
> *I noticed that Dan was erratic in attending classes. However, whenever he did do so, he came across as brilliant. He was good at critical analyses and was innovative in his approach in solving business problems. In short, he stood out in the class as an intellectual outlier. All the professors noticed this quality in him. However, all of them also rued the fact that he was tardy and lacked sincerity when it came to academics. As faculty teaching the cohort a couple of subjects and also the dean in which this program was housed, I had to attend to the matter. In fact his case first came to light over a disciplinary matter in which he was involved. After a few meetings and enquiring about his activities from his classmates, it was clear that Dan was dealing with some issues. He would lock himself up in the room for days together, ordering in meals instead of going to the common dining place.*

Also he would be found sleeping for long spells of time. Despite his friends stopping by his dorm room to cajole him to attend classes or join them to hang out, he continued to avoid.

When I met Dan, he had this vacant look. I enquired about his well-being, but his answers were evasive. I also enquired about his family. I kept up with these sessions and discovered that the pressure of performance that he'd undergone in his childhood through adolescence and adulthood had finally caught up with him. The problem lay in his mortal fear of failing his family. Dan's illustrious family, its expectations, the constant unseen burden of 'delivering' against those expectations had resulted in him experimenting with psychotropic drugs. This explained everything. Once again as with Nyla, we began counselling him and bringing him out of his emotional stress.

Eventually, Dan got through the program and secured one of the best jobs on campus. He rid himself of drug dependency (while on campus) and now works in a Big Four Consulting Firm.

Another case that I recall is that of Zed, a millennial who went through considerable anxiety and trauma. This was sometime in 2004-05. His/her stress was of a different kind.

One day I received an email from Zed asking me about my views on gays. I call him Zed because there was no way of knowing the gender. At that time homosexuality was a crime punishable by law in India. Coming out was unimaginable. Intolerance began with family members and continued into other social institutions.

Despite the larger social antipathy towards the LGBTQ community Gay Pride Walks, gay literature, mainstreaming of the communities in mass media was on the rise around the same time. Social networking sites were doing their bit to make these communities feel comfortable and taboos were being questioned more vociferously than before.

Perhaps the email was directed to me because I took classes in Human Resource Management and was teaching concepts like Equal Opportunity, Affirmative Action, Diversity, and Compensation in organizations. I surmised that Zed was fearful that if his/her preference was discovered, how would the employers view this?

Zed continued sending me emails detailing various social situations and stories and asking me for my opinion on matters 'gay.' There were questions about why classmates snickered (bullied) at someone who was gay or at least overtly appeared gay. In another mail, I was asked whether company managements discriminated if they found out that a person was gay and so on.

The emails and the situations described in them were fairly anonymized, even so, I was not in a position to respond to such emails due to prevailing rules of conduct and security at the university. However, I wondered what the person was actually going through emotionally, leading a furtive life in the closet.

I am left with a sad feeling of not being able to help Zed. If it had been today, when the law in favor of recognizing LGBTQs and LGBTQ unions has been passed in India, I would have been able to provide some help to a troubled soul.

Stress is an illness that has hit the millennial generation far ahead of their earlier generational counterparts. There are several reasons for stress being an indivisible part of their waking lives. They are awake long hours, cheat on sleep, hence waking lives, in the literal sense of the word. The fear of failure, intense competition, parental expectations or simply the desire to excel have kept the millennials on their toes 24/7. Add to this one more reason, gender. To be a millennial and a female made for a potent recipe for being more stressed. The World Health Organization[20] pegs harassment and bullying as causes for mental health issues, especially among LGBTQ, racial minorities and women.

Talking of women, the story of Sheila rings true of practically any talented, versatile and motivated woman who have faced the pressure of being female in a male dominated industry. The only difference is that it continues to exist despite so much progress in equal rights and affirmative action.

---

[20] Hillary Hoffower, Allana Akhtar (2019). Lonely, burned out, and depressed: The state of millennials' mental health in 2019. OCT 10, 2019, 17:00 IST. https://www.businessinsider.in/slideshows/miscellaneous/lonely-burned-out-and-depressed-the-state-of-millennials-mental-health-in-2019/slidelist/71521961.cms#slideid=71521977

Sheila's stress was personal for me, as year in and year out, when the hiring season came up, I found a few girl students getting a bad deal from even reputed companies. Profiling the jobs to keep out female aspirants was subtle. Limiting the vacancies, and job trimming were common excuses for reducing their chances at competing. I went out of my way to ensure that the girls got a fair chance at competing and receiving the opportunity to serve in top companies in the built environment.

Sheila was one of my brightest students who had enrolled in one of our programs after her bachelor's degree in architecture. She had some of the best grades right from her school days, through college, and she continued with the same consistency in the master's program. She had earned prestigious scholarships that were difficult to win from her school and college days. She graduated from our university with the 'Institute Gold Medal' for academic excellence from among hundreds of students.

Being a millennial and brought up in affluence with doting parents and brother, she was never in want of anything. Her life's goals and daily routines had been well laid out and her family played an integral role in her achievements. She was 'perfect,' always cheerful, kind, ambitious, with a never-say-die attitude. She was at the forefront of the university's outreach initiatives with industry, social services, and cultural activities. She displayed remarkable leadership skills in the various responsibilities and positions she held. Not only was she good at academics she was also generous enough to regularly hold coaching sessions for her classmates. She helped them with their queries and conceptual challenges in diverse courses like econometrics and organizational behavior, with equal facility. In short, she was what any academic management would consider an ideal or dream student to admit.

Towards the end of the program, as the recruiting companies started coming to the campus, a strange thing happened. Shortlists came out without her name on them. Many bluechip and reputed multinational companies operating in India and overseas, who are known to be finicky about high grades, strangely passed her on for students with comparatively lesser scores.

For those few companies that did shortlist her, her name was conspicuous by its absence in the final selection list, despite topping the written tests and giving a good performance in the discussion and interview rounds. This was disconcerting. Even those students who had competed with Sheila in the discussion and interview rounds, were perplexed and often felt guilty that they were being chosen over her. Once again, as her faculty and dean of the program, it did not seem right that one of the brightest and best students on the campus was being passed over with no logical explanation for it. Post mortems of the process with the employment search team did not yield any convincing answers.

One day I was having a discussion with Sheila about her plans to crack the selection code. I asked her to reflect on the final selected candidates where she was certain of being offered a position. One by one we started going over the firms and matching them with the final selections that they had made. A pattern began emerging. Most of the companies had chosen all male teams in the final rounds. In the one odd case where a female student had made it to the final list, the position had a 'soft' profile, e.g. planning or human resources. All the profiles which required visiting or working at building or infrastructure project sites, or which needed constant travel had 'all male' teams. It was clear that Sheila was not considered appropriate for the job despite being qualified and also being willing to work in the profile. This was perhaps one of the rare moments when Sheila questioned the tacit 'discrimination' she was having to face due to her gender. It was sad to see her not being given the fruit of her efforts and was being prevented from competing on an equal footing.

Sheila needed some counselling to restore her usual joie de vivre. When I look back at my own times and the similar difficulties that I faced as a female student, it saddens me that despite decades going by little seemed to have changed. The only difference is that as Gen X, we took this as a given and learned to work around it. Our mothers, sisters, and grandmothers had all faced discrimination. Our coping mechanisms to deal with it were different.

How was I to explain this to Sheila, who had been brought up with no bias related to gender, who'd been encouraged to believe that she could reach for the stars and nothing was ever going to stop her from making her dreams come true? She was a prima donna, and to be fair to her she had even proven that she had it in her. To be rudely awakened and being made to realize that she would not be part of a particular club by the macho construction organizations was not a normal 'rite of passage' that Sheila, a millennial, needed to go through.

The indignation that I witnessed among other female students but equally so among male students for Sheila's cause, was definitely heartening to see. Male students came out in good numbers to express solidarity with their female counterparts. Over a period of time, this collective indignation resulted in the university management taking up the issue of equal opportunities and inclusivity with the recruiting companies.

It resulted in a lot of exchanges with companies to dissuade them from exhibiting any form of discrimination, overt or covert, during recruitments at the university. Counselling for the placement officers and policies were put in place to avoid companies with such 'masculine' inclinations that blatantly thwarted inclusivity. Over a period of time green shoots of change started appearing. The so-called male centric jobs like site managers are now accessible to female students and to my satisfaction, they are swinging them.

The stories of *Nyla, Dan, Zed, and Sheila* are symbolic of numerous such stories and their variants being played out every day on campuses and elsewhere in the world.

The millennial psyche is fragile, according to Jean Twenge[21] an American psychologist, who researches generational differences. Could this be attributed to the generation's early start with the internet? Millennials were the first ones to experience the good, bad, and ugly served by the internet.

To my mind, with this generation, relationships burst outward from the limited family and community circles into the big, wide world. With Baby Boomers/Gen Xers, if there were deviations in behaviors either at home or at school, private censure was the common way of tackling

---

[21] Twenge, J. M. (2011). Generational differences in mental health: Are children and adolescents suffering more, or less? *American Journal of Orthopsychiatry, 81*(4), 469–472. https://doi.org/10.1111/j.1939-0025.2011.01115.x

misdemeanors. With internet and social networking sites there arose a new fear, a fear of recrimination from the aggrieved party in a rather public manner.

Overnight complete strangers could become part of a conversation that seemed boundless in its scope. There was also the fear of embarrassment and shame that accompanies socially awkward situations. The thumbs down, trolling or derogatory posts were the unpleasant side effects of being continuously plugged into this virtual world. The millennials had to metamorphose into adolescence or adulthood wrought with the fear of committing social faux pas and pitfalls in front of unknown virtual entities. While most learned to steer clear of controversies, some coped by creating virtual avatars unlike their real selves, while the meek were left emotionally singed and scarred.

In this world, there are many benefits of all things rational, though it is for us to counter the pitfalls of excessive rationalism with moderation, wisdom and also spiritualism. In their growing up years most millennials unlike their Gen X and Baby Boomer counterparts had been bereft of the make belief world of fairies, gnomes, pixies, and goblins. The movement had grown in favor of weaning children away from fantasy towards realism. The new ideas that had taken root in the 1990s and continued into the millennium revolved around teaching children to face reality rather than masking it behind imaginary characters. The new thought was that fantasy unconsciously promoted escapism, notwithstanding other issues such as gender inequality and stereotypes, through its historically prejudiced content. Further criticism of the fairy tales included, the unfailing depiction of slim, willowy women, with porcelain white skin, who always looked beautiful. Without going further on, it will suffice to know that in the absence of fantasy these kids mostly grew up with content that was realistic and humdrum. Thank God, many years later the *Harry Potter* series hit the stands and made fantasy a hero once again.

On the surface, it appeared that fairy tales had provided a means of succor to a whole generation in coping with their lives. This very escape into an imaginary world, processing the 'evils' and the 'injustices' and emerging with solutions to face one's own reality was a useful tool in providing directions. It was always the good overcoming evil, or the kind and courageous ultimately winning the prize, and the beastly and cruel turning into dust for their bad ways. Somehow the fairy tales sounded a lot like what the parents told at home, the teachers in school and the priest in the temple. Coping became easier as fantasy was being endorsed by the immediate environment. With the advent of the internet, information was ubiquitous. When Gen X parents attempted to explain phenomena using fantasy, they were immediately stopped by the young millennials as it was not in accordance with what was explained elsewhere!

With the internet it also meant there is no escaping the constant and incessant strobe lights on one's persona. This attention does little good when it comes to managing one's self esteem or anxieties. At least according to Jenny Marie in a NAMI[22] article in which she shares her millennial daughter's confession of experiencing anxiety and stress due to social media. In this scenario, feelings of insecurity abound. According to Marie the peculiar 'sense of immediacy—everything has to happen right away, at the click of a button' puts pressure to constantly monitor one's virtual image and make it as perfect as possible, acting as if you are the most sorted individual on earth, while privately having misgivings about it. It ends in believing that strangers have the true hang of the situation which is even more than the persons around you. Does this make the whole situation delusional for the millennials?

Social media is virtual, families and communities are real. However, the incredible connectedness and constancy of the virtual alters young minds into thinking that the virtual is *'real'*. This disconnectedness with the actual context plays itself out adversely when faced with real life circumstances that are difficult to cope with, such as when there are fewer jobs on offer, lower pay packages, and slower career growth. It is also this obsessive desire to be perfect which leads millennials to therapy when at some point the mirror cracks.

This is also borne out by the increasing number of university students the world over seeking psychological counsellors to help manage stress and for eliminating suicidal thoughts. So also, is the case with young millennials employed in large corporations who find an urge to seek out the organizations' counselling facilities a lot more frequently than their predecessor generations. Stress leads to physiological problems like

---

22 Jenny Marie Blog (2019). Millennials and Mental Health. See: https://www.nami.org/Blogs/NAMI-Blog/February-2019/Millennials-and-Mental-Health Copyright © 2020 NAMI.

binge eating followed by guilt, substance dependence, obesity and body complex, and diabetes and hypertension afflicting them as early as in their mid-20s and 30s[23]. The real problem arises when one's self worth is allowed to be determined by others.

I would term it as 'The *Perfect* Problem'. The tendency to push oneself to the extreme to look, act, sound and be perfect, which comes not so much from an inner desire to be that way but which is driven by an external force. If it isn't natural, the effort in maintaining the contrived persona is very high. Over a period of time, the dichotomy of what you aren't but what you have projected to the world chains you to the act. This is what takes a massive mental and emotional toll, scarring the psyche permanently in extreme cases.

Another psychological affliction that millennials confess to, is the feeling of loneliness. Some even call them the loneliest generation ever. A study found that 30 percent of the surveyed sample of millennials in the US said they always or often felt lonely compared to 20 percent Gen X members. In the same survey, most of millennials confessed to not having acquaintances, friends, close friends, or best friends[24].

Extreme cases of stress result in early burnouts. These burnouts can be attributed to rising workloads, less staff and resources, and long working hours. Government agencies and psychotherapy pundits, spiritual gurus, fitness coaches, nutritional advisors, suggest embracing mindfulness, meditation, binaural sounds, detoxification remedies like turning off social media, quitting coffee and sugar, doing meditation and exercise as solutions.

Happily there is increasing talk of wellness coming from younger generations than ever before[25]. Perhaps they have seen the excessive

---

23 Brooke Donatone (2014). Why are so many millennials depressed? A therapist points the finger at Mom and Dad. See: https://www.washingtonpost.com/national/health-science/why-are-so-many-millennials-depressed-a-therapist-points-the-finger-at-mom-and-dad/2014/01/06/19f4f1c4-69a1-11e3-8b5b-a77187b716a3_story.html

24 Hillary Hoffower and Allana Akhtar (2019). Lonely, burned out, and depressed: The state of millennials' mental health. See: https://www.businessinsider.in/strategy/news/lonely-burned-out-and-depressed-the-state-of-millennials-mental-health-in-2019/articleshow/71521984.cms

25 Katherine Schreiber (2016). 5 Reasons You're Stressed AF — and How to Deal Why too many twentysomethings still #CantEven. MAR 22, 2016. https://www.cosmopolitan.com/health-fitness/a55553/millennial-stress-depression-anxiety/

workloads and struggles of their Gen X parents, having been *'home alone'* far too often while growing up. In fact, when it comes to raising children, most of the millennials prefer postponing having children than staring at the reality of not being around for them. They tend to postpone responsibilities for reasons other than financial. Having said that, the majority perceive themselves as not ready to take on life's complexities.

I recall a conversation I had sometime in 2007, with a Chinese friend and fellow academic in Guangzhou University, Cathy Wu, who lives in Guangzhou.

> *Cathy Wu's daughter, Jian, is a typical millennial. She was then 30- years-old. She had been staying in another city since her teens, first due to her education and thereafter for her job. However, within a few months of joining a firm, Jian was back home for a number of reasons.*
>
> *When she accepted the offer, Jian was upbeat because she was chosen from an accomplished and experienced pool of competitors. Being in the design field and having undergone a very expensive master's program from a top school, her Gen X parents were happy that their child was on the right track in her career, and had encouraged her all along. Jian's reasons for quitting were interesting. For one, she was unable to cope with office politics. She was perplexed by the overt hostility of her older colleagues towards her. Second, the money she was getting was far too little to allow her to use even basic services such as cleaning and laundry that she had been accustomed to since her childhood. And third, she admitted that even if she had coped with this, her long hours made her discontented as she was unable to find the balance between work and leisure. At the same time, the fear of intellectual stagnation petrified her.*
>
> *Low pay meant making meals at home which she had no time for and frankly was not very adept at, either. They were a typical comfortable, one child, middle-class family with Cathy a professor in construction management at the Guangzhou university and her dad a businessman. Jian never was required to help at home, because housekeepers were always around to manage. Moreover, the two sets of grandparents also flipped in and out of the house often.*

Back home with her parents, Jian decided that she would enroll in a doctoral program which would enable her to diversify her interests. She acquired a doctorate but was yet to be employed meaningfully, and was engaged with part time gigs with colleges and think tanks while she continued to stay with her parents. When Cathy asked Jian what her future plans were, she merely shrugged as if to say 'I'll take that as it comes'.

An article in *Time* magazine,[26] talks about how millennials find it difficult to take firm decisions and refers to them as those who 'would rather hike in the Himalayas than climb a corporate ladder.' Jian's story is as much that of not knowing how to 'grow up' and taking decisions, as much as it about appears to be a millennial not wanting to take responsibility of her own life.

Millennials and the Competition Gene

Experts and research studies have been quoted to elicit the important nuances that typify the millennial psyche. While more on workplace related issues of millennials follows in the next chapter, in this section emphasis on the emotional make up related to competition is elaborated. The millennial personality appears less enamored by the idea of ruthless competitiveness, and charismatic leadership in particular. This is in stark contrast to the Gen Xer/Baby Boomer generation where individual, macho leadership was central at personal, organizational and global levels.

Sam Hill (a Newsweek contributor, consultant, and best-selling author), contends that millennials do not seem as inspired as the Baby Boomers were, in their contemporary times. He compares the millennials to the Baby Boomers which according to him was the 'best ever' generation. He talks about the narrow definition of ambition that millennials tend to have. For example, the workplace priorities that keep millennials preoccupied lie in the realms of personal health insurance, child care, student loans, and paid family leave. In contrast, the Baby Boomers/Gen X's priorities were the workplace itself! This helped usher in enormous gains for humankind enabling workplaces to become fairer and safer.

---

[26] 12 David M. Gross and Sophfronia Scott (2001). Proceeding with Caution http://content.time.com/time/magazine/article/0,9171,155010,00.html

Some of these massive movements were led by the earlier generation through its involvement in civil rights, apartheid, volunteering, and doing research for the general good.

Another report produced by Deloitte-GreenHouse in 2017, described the millennial workplace mindset and came up with very interesting findings. Its dataset was large comprising of 19,568 millennials surveyed during 2013-16 in areas related to personality, career aspirations, priorities (ambitions), and stress and coping mechanisms. As we know the millennial generation has been described by several appellations such as the 'me-gen', the 'self-absorbed' or 'narcissistic' generation. However, the findings of the Deloitte- Greenhouse report, revealed something to the contrary. The majority of the participants were found to be risk -averse, which the study classified as the 'Guardian Personality' type. The Guardian Personality types were characterized by traits of being methodical, reserved, detail-oriented, practical, structured, and loyal.

I shall describe how this interesting finding played out for me within my students, much before the survey report was out.

In my years in academia, I saw very few bitter acrimonies and disagreements among the students when it came to competing for jobs, organizing important events or doing group assignments in class. I found that pretty surprising as from my point of view, they appeared seriously devoid of the competitive spirit. As I had explained in the earlier on in the book, in my own experience as a Gen Xer, competition was something we were taught to 'devour for breakfast'.

In the new decade of the millennium, while continuing work with my students, I found myself being more ambitious for the students than they appeared to be for themselves. Whether it was intercollegiate or inter B-school competitions, or within the institute, when it came to competing, I found them less inclined to go the whole hog. It was always a case of a *"We'll try, let's see what happens"*, attitude. When it came to jobs too, they would help each other as much as possible to get to the finish line. Much like Sheila who was always there for her classmates. There were countless occasions when they came to me and openly admitted that someone else deserved to get the job instead of them. I found these admissions though genuine, very strange.

Moreso as the same lack luster approach to winning (as it appeared to me then) was simultaneously being played out at home.

My younger son was a decent track athlete in school and was top draw when it came to winning individual events. In keeping up with our duty as parents, we paid close attention to him as the tournaments drew closer. It entailed a closer supervision of his meals, practice sessions, and mental grit. We spoke to him about the pressure of the expectations he carried on his slim shoulders to uphold the school's sporting honor, expectations of his peers and friends, and all those who were looking forward to him winning the medals. We explained to him that while that was important it was more important to keep a keen eye on the competitor and play the game to win, as much as possible. We thought that this drumming would perhaps translate into a rush of competitive adrenaline. We discussed game plans and counter moves with scenarios to prepare him for the competitions. In short, we tried to awaken his killer instinct to win.

To our surprise he would always protest when we said anything that sounded like it was thwarting the values of sportsmanship, friendship and goodwill. In the very rare event that he came home with the silver or the bronze, he never attributed it to any unfair practice, bad form or even bad luck. He always said he was happy for the person who had won as on that day the other boy was a better man. I found this truly strange, for as Gen Xers we had been raised to always be ready for a fight, unto the last. In our growing up years we were constantly reminded of how 'life is not easy; one needed to fight for one's place in the sun.'

This boy never appeared delirious with joy even in triumph, which to our minds he richly deserved to be. Instead I always found him going over and consoling his compatriots who'd lost the races. He never seemed to correlate his wins with the defeat of others. It was always team play. I never failed to put in an appearance on the day of the tournament and keenly observed the other kids who'd won different races. Not too many appeared haughty in victory. Much like the tempered millennials, Federer or Djokovic who always come across humble and dignified in victory or defeat.

There appears to me a strange kind of '*ubuntu*[27]' among millennials, who believe in taking as many as possible along in their journey, in stark contrast to the fierce competitiveness of our times. Like in the case of my athlete son, I knew that most times they were capable of far more than what they pitched for, however they were not averse to abdicate their own success in favor of a better performer.

The only plausible reasons for such behavior could be that though talented and erudite, they lacked the instincts of being outgoing, spontaneous, risk-seeking, and imaginative. These are also the characteristics of the 'Pioneers' described in the Deloitte-Greenhouse report. Only 18 percent of the millennials were in the Pioneers cohort as compared to 26 percent among the Gen Xers.

However, I am not fully convinced they can be so devoid of these instincts. Competition and cooperation are natural instincts and my bet is that competition exists but, in a form, and manner Gen Xers are yet to fully unearth.

27 is a Zulu word which means 'a quality that includes the essential human virtues; compassion and humanity'.

CHAPTER 5

Millennials and the Workplace

MILLENNIALS AT WORK

According to Pew Research millennials in the US became the single largest segment among all generations active in the workforce in 2016.[28] Therefore, it is not surprising that more focus to better understand the millennials' engagement drivers is in line. Research and leading consulting firms tracking generational viewpoints, unearth millennials' characteristics, the values that set them apart, their inherent quirks, the peculiar circumstances that surround them, and their overall outlook towards life.

Further reading throws light, metaphorically, on the manner in which millennials have come to 'inhabit' their work spaces. What you might find are traditional biases held by different older age groups in the workplaces. Often these biases could color viewpoints even before the millennials have had a chance to be understood or to prove themselves. In turn millennials feel piqued by this colored view, ending up in push backs or simply exiting organizations. Forward looking organizations have taken this workplace 'bias' on board and have established sensitivity training for getting generations to work together harmoniously towards organizational goals. Some organizations that have taken steps in this direction are Google, NetSuite, the US Army, Uber, Sephora, and Banana Republic.

---

[28] Richard Fry (2018). Millennials are the largest generation in the U.S. labor force. https://www.pewresearch.org/fact-tank/2018/04/11/millennials-largest-generation-us-labor-force/

Here's how this played out for me in the academic world, though not exactly like the rest of the private and public institutions that have their share of generational angst.

With millennials it was commonplace for me to take agitated phone calls, or have morose ex-students sit before me, off-loading the emotionally unsatisfying incidences of their work lives. I recall scores of incidents when within a couple of months of joining companies after graduation there was discontent. Their pet peeve was how the *'oldies'* in the company, continued to insist on retaining 'obsolete' ways of working. Some of the bosses were even unwilling to accept suggestions from the millennials for improving efficiency by introducing contemporary, agile processes or technology. In most cases they faced sustained and continuous resistance.

According to millennial Keevin O'Rourke,[29] millennials love autonomy and meaningful contributions in the workplace. For them, rising up the corporate ladder and getting fat pay cheques is not a bigger goal than being given the freedom to do the job independently and getting to choose their own teams. This way they find more meaning in what they are doing and consider it time well spent. As a matter of fact, disengagement sets in when this aspect is missing from their work lives.

Many rued the fact that they had to 'unlearn' important tools and techniques they'd learned while at the university, and some parts of their learning inventory when they joined organizations. For example, I clearly remember the millennials grumbling about their tussles with their bosses who resisted the use of contemporary specialized software and wanted to continue with solutions in basic software or none at all!

In other instances, the new millennial recruits faced animosity and non-cooperation from the older incumbents on vague and generic grounds of '*it doesn't happen your way kid, we've done it this way for years, that's the way it will be, shape up or ship out*.' This kind of a vibe that went around, did little to help the millennials feel at ease in their companies, let alone develop a feeling of loyalty or attachment. They tended to feel undermined.

---

[29] Keevin O'Rourke (May 11, 2015). How to Make Millennials Want to Work for You. Copyright TEDxUNI. https://www.youtube.com/watch?v=QhOqki06IGo

Every year I was privy to this feedback from my students and every year I had to lend them an ear, offer suggestions, and simply hope that they would be able to tide over these situations with time. Sadly, the highest turnover of jobs after campus recruitments happened in the first couple of months to a year of our graduating cohorts joining companies. There appeared no simple way to put a finger in the dyke to help the cause. If magnified over the larger recruitment landscape this was nothing but a huge waste of resources for organizations and a source of heartburn for the millennials.

The third dimension to this mismatch was the academic institutions. Academic institutions act as facilitators in the recruitments. They frequently face flak from companies which give feedback on the new recruits. This feedback would cover the inability of the new recruits to 'adjust' to the prevailing corporate culture. The allegation being that academic institutions are not instilling 'proper' values of the importance of blending, identifying and internalizing corporate philosophies, among the student cohorts. In other words, teaching them the importance of loyalty. A new recruit leaving the organization within short periods after joining raises questions internally for the HR departments, as it entails costs of the recruitment, suitability of the candidates and thorough checks of the willingness of the recruit to stay with the company for a reasonable period of time.

Needless to say, the situation helped none of the stakeholders. I decided that something needed to be done. One of the solutions for avoiding early exits from companies was to have a 'winding down' session with the outgoing class. One could say a la mode of the highly feted and followed book *What They Don't Teach You at Harvard Business School: Notes from a Street-Smart Executive* by Mark McCormack.[30]

When I reflected on my early days in the industry, armed with a business management master's degree, I realized we were a far cry from these highly impatient and bemused millennials with a similar degree. It would be untrue if I said as young employees, we were the embodiment of patience. We too showed angst against the earlier generation managers. Like the millennials, we too could have had more experienced (but not always formally qualified executives) in our workplaces, we felt

[30] Mark H. McCormack (1986). What They Don't Teach You at Harvard Business School: Notes from a Street-Smart Executive. Bantam Trade Paperback.

frustrated with their set ways. Moreover, they could be crabby too. All generations feel this way with the older. It was just that we were not too overly hung up with our situation, as we were taught to train our focus on job performance. We knew that eventually *'this too shall pass'*. We did not feel the necessity to leave our jobs, though at most we may have sought transfers. Maybe we could be classified as the '*somewhat*' impatient and not the '*highly*' impatient kinds of employees? By way of further explanation, it could be that Gen X came into the mainstream at a different time. Gen X members the workplace were docile in front of their seniors due to the high emphasis on respect for elders, more or less common across all cultures. Hence, we were more likely to 'hero worship' and revere senior executives.

Coming back to the millennial students at the university, the frustration and anxiety that simmered in them affected me greatly. It was not so much a specific instance or a particular person who went through problems, it actually pointed to a prevailing generic tendency. As an academic I could see clearly that this mismatch affected not only the organizations' processes but also the psyche of the millennials who were facing issues on a day to day basis. By now it was amply evident to me that the millennials inwardly struggled to be treated as equals, though outwardly they displayed a certain devil-may-care 'swag.' They were aware of the effect they had on their bosses, organization, and teams. Beneath the swag, they were no less ambitious than their predecessors.

I decided to understand why senior managements of organizations tended to dismiss the incoming millennials either as upstarts or mere green horns.

POPULAR NOTIONS AND STEREOTYPES HAUNTING MILLENNIALS IN THE WORKPLACE

Lazy and entitled

Not entirely true!

Millennials are fiercely ambitious and hence likely to be the most stressed. This is contrary to earlier surveys which plugged them as a lazy, laid back, leisure seeking lot. According to psychologists the compulsion to keep accumulating accolades was perhaps the reason for this. Since their early childhood, millennials were taught to excel in various activities. When one wins accolades, the success hormones (dopamine, oxytocin, serotonin, and endorphin), are released in the brain, which act as a natural stimulant for feeling happy and motivated to do more. This, in turn propels more acts for seeking appreciation or success.

According to Timothy A. Judge (2009)[31] ambition is correlated to educational attainments, occupation prestige, and income. This is the good side of being ambitious. However, Judge also found a weak correlation between ambition and life satisfaction. For millennials, ambition and mental stress are high. This leads to lowered satisfaction due to a work-life imbalance. A 2019 study on their preferences and priorities by Deloitte[32] indirectly attributed stress to shrunk opportunities in employment.

The deficit in the availability of steady and meaningful jobs has affected the millennials' ability to make meaningful life choices. Catastrophic economic crises hit some countries, particularly the US, which professionally impacted the millennials the most. The early cohorts joined the workforce close to or soon after the economic recession of 9/11 in the new millennium, and later entrants were hit by the 2008 financial crisis. The 2008, Great Financial Crisis (GFC) as it has come to be known, carried across the Atlantic affecting European countries, and onward, casting a pall of gloom over the whole world. Though well qualified, there were fewer opportunities for millennials for securing full-time employment. Gig working increased in these countries partially due to the inability to get jobs and partially by choice. The 2008 recession was very deep and countries all over the world have been grappling with improving economic growth for over a decade of this millennium.

Many pundits love to call it the most blighted generation as crisis upon crisis hits the world. The millennials are a generation that was buffeted

---

31 Judge T., Kammeyer-Mueller J. (2009). On the Value of Aiming High: The Causes and Consequences of Ambition, Journal of Applied Psychology. http://www.timothy-judge.com/documents/Ambition-JAPINPRESS.pdf

32 The Deloitte Global Millennial Survey (2019). Optimism, trust reach troubling low levels. https://www2.deloitte.com/cn/en/pages/about-deloitte/articles/2019-millennial-survey.html

time and again with economic setbacks. As mentioned earlier, the oldest of the cohort reached adulthood when 9/11 happened and wiped out quite a few jobs in the US labor market. The GFC further undermined economic recovery leaving them with lower wage levels.

To add to the economic crises around the world, the novel corona virus pandemic (COVID-19) in 2020, was so maleficent that it wiped out entire countries' economic worth and wealth indiscriminately across the globe. COVID-19 pandemic, further pushed millennials into the ground. Some economic experts feared that this generation, at least in the US, could perhaps never recover from this enough to secure themselves comfortably over their lifetimes. Millennial earnings have reduced drastically. Compared to the Gen Xers, millennials are not in a position to acquire wealth and assets at the pace their predecessor generations were able to accumulate.

It is a strange case never seen in the world before, where highly qualified individuals are found struggling to stay in employment.

These series of disasters, happening over the past two decades, led to pushing back the clock of economic and social progress around the world. The ramifications of these losses can be compared to the difficult decades that the Greatest Generation had to suffer between 1919 - 1945.[33]

To understand their circumstances better, a comparison with earlier generational counterparts, the Baby Boomers and Gen X, would be relevant. At the time of their coming of age, they had far more job opportunities for the asking. On the other hand, the millennials had lower real incomes, fewer assets, and higher education debts as they entered the workforce. As if this was not enough, there were not many jobs left to scrape out from the pan. In situations like this, it is difficult for millennials to recover their true economic worth through fair wages even over a lifetime. The majority of millennials are likely to have the worst wealth generating capabilities. Their ability to meet their lifetime goals too is now under severe threat. This could result in unfair comparisons in the performance of the millennials. Gen X could well be colored in

---

[33] The Greatest Generation (persons born between 1901-24), saw two World Wars, the Spanish plague, and the Great Depression of 1929-39.

its judgment when it comes to assessing the real contribution of the millennials to organizational goals. To my mind Gen X bosses may be involuntarily holding their early career experiences as the yardstick for measuring the millennial workforce's performance.

I tend to carry a different perspective.

To me, the constant turbulence that has befallen millennials on the back of economic, social and health crises, the long drawn gloomy economic specter, require loads of courage to emerge triumphant.

A good deal of patience in assessing their true capabilities and contribution would be needed given the extraordinary global times in which they attained adulthood and began their work lives.

Lack loyalty, frequent job hoppers

Initial data published in the early decade of the millennium, gave rise to the impression that the millennials were flighty when it came to jobs; 57 percent of the millennials were found to have retention issues of some kind.[34] Further, unlike their Gen X counterparts who valued longevity, millennials actively tended to seek job changes, far often and far too rapidly. However, recent meta-data and trends observed by the largest professional search engine LinkedIn points otherwise. LinkedIn studies have found no difference in the work ethics of different generations. The millennials have the same propensity to be loyal and identify with a company's priorities as any other preceding generation. What stands out for the millennials is the importance they ascribe to certain aspects of the work that they do. They are likely to leave only if they do not find the three important things, they hold dear, viz. career advancement opportunities, better pay and challenging work.[35]

A significant departure from the earlier generations is the millennials' desire to improve the *qualitative* aspects of their work life. This aspect holds

---

34 Millennials Are Changing the Way We Do Performance Reviews. https://www.theoverturegroup.com/blog/millennials-are-changing-the-way-we-do-performance-reviews

35 LinkedIn Releases New Data on Millennials [Infographic]. https://www.socialmediatoday.com/social-business/linkedin-releases-new-data-millennials-infographic

a greater significance for millennials compared to earlier generations. For example, the boss' ability to be ethical, fair, transparent, and consistent. They ascribe far more value and importance to these qualities, than to a boss who simply appreciates task related accomplishments. Millennials love transparency and consistency. A vast majority of millennials regard non-transparent performance appraisal systems with doubt. In a study by TriNet,[36] 74 percent of the participants very often felt that their managers and peers kept them 'in the dark' about how they thought the millennials were performing, at work. The same study also found that this led millennials to have misgivings about their abilities to perform future tasks.

For millennials working for a company with a conscience is of more than normal importance. The millennials are a socially and environmentally conscious generation. They are most likely to first search the internet about a company's green conscience and its corporate social initiatives before accepting the employment offer. A report carried in *Livemint*[37] on Indian millennial job seekers, listed 'making a positive impact on society and community' as the top- most job priority for 57 percent of the millennials!

The Netizens are known to be particularly squeamish when it comes to issues of data privacy and security. They are more likely to take a dim view of organizations which do not explicitly show sensitivity to this aspect. In reality, they are less likely to join if they come across breach and abuse of privacy rights by companies.

All in all, it would be perilous to box millennials into the traditional work values of the Baby Boomers and Gen Xers in workplaces, the latter were far more conforming in their approach. Contrary to this, millennials prefer more clarity in roles, relevant feedback and a strong sense of purpose to keep them going.

---

[36] Millennials Are Changing the Way We Do Performance Reviews. https://www.theoverturegroup.com/blog/millennials-are-changing-the-way-we-do-performance-reviews

[37] Lata Jha (2019). What really matters to Millennials, Gen Z. https://www.livemint.com/news/india/what-really-matters-to-millennials-gen-z-1561573198602.html

Millennials do not have strong work ethics

A study by the Center of Generational Kinesics[38] (CGK) found that 44 percent of the millennials expected a raise within one year of starting a job. Most organizations find this aspect irksome. I have mentioned earlier how most of the millennial cohort had relatively higher levels of educational attainment, enjoyed a better quality of life in their growing up years, were highly networked, and of course were an acutely aware generation than any before. All this has enabled them to make comparisons between companies, persons, and situations far more quickly based on the information they access. This captiousness is observed substantially more among them than in their senior counterparts. Perhaps the vast amount of data available on the internet has made millennials more circumspect about whom they wish to work for. When it comes to job profiles compromising is less preferred when millennials perceive that options suitable to their learning and competencies are available. They are more likely to negotiate a profile that plays to their personal and technical strengths. This focus on being treated fairly at the workplace and feeling disgruntled if they are not, makes them less willing to work in organizations they perceive as not subscribing to those standards.

With earlier generations, the corporate culture consciously promoted adherence to family values. Throughout the 1960s, '70s and '80s house magazines were a common unifying feature used by large scale companies to bond with employees and their families. Multifarious schemes were part of employee engagement initiatives. It was typical to have company sponsored family outings, or parties and scholarships for meritorious children publicized through house magazines and newsletters. What's more, family members of Baby Boomer/Gen X executives raved about the frequent flyer miles their parents notched up as globe-trotting executives. Somehow this was an indicator to underscore the power and status executives commanded at work. To be referred to as a 'high flying executive' was a trophy. For the high- flying executive, cancelling or postponing vacations further underscored this point. So much so that it was considered aspirational to work for companies that provided opportunities to move higher in the organizational ladder even when it

[38] Jason Dorsey, Millennials understand money better than you think. https://genhq.com/millennials-understand-money-better-think/. Copyright CGK 2020.

led to reduced time for personal and family involvement. Back then it was considered an acceptable collateral for one's professional growth. Fat pay cheques, bonuses and perquisites far outweighed other considerations. Above all the chance to wield power gave a heady high.

No one complained against this happy burden that high flying executives carried on their shoulders. On the other hand, the world that the millennials stepped into was difficult, almost from the word go. The economic crises led to millennials not being remunerated as well as their antecessors. This is why millennials feel a sense of outrage and indignance over the growing inequities in remuneration and work life balance.

At this point it is important to know that millennials are tuned into others. On an average, one-third of the millennials donate to a charity or a non-profit or offer volunteer work or do internships. This leads one to believe that for the millennials, investing in volunteering carries the same significance as investing in family time and well -being. According to experts Michael Hias and Morely Winograd,[39] in the workplaces too it might well be that team or collective welfare is most likely to take center stage vis-à-vis individual success. It is when millennials perceive a unreasonable disparity among the various levels of the hierarchy that there is a strong likelihood of dissonance creeping in.

Gen X was known to adopt a work ethic involving long hours and long-lived loyalties to their organizations. Undying fealty to corporations is now a thing of the past. What was representative in the earlier generations will no longer be in evidence going forward. With more millennials joining the workforce it is a given that organizations will be compelled to reconcile all debates on matters of significance to millennials, before expecting higher degrees of loyalty from them.

Millennials more emotions driven, less professional?

I tend to carry this impression which is also fairly well represented in my generation, that millennials possess certain emotional frames of reference at the collective level, quite unique to them. To many of us, millennials come across as gentler and more generous in their attitudes.

---

[39] Danielle Shoots (2018). Millennials were Born to Lead, Here's Why. TEDxMilehigh. https://www.youtube.com/watch?v=D8E-EcvjDOM

They appear less willing to walk over something or somebody to reach their individual objectives. On this matter seniors privately conclude that they lack aggression and dynamism; qualities considered important and to be displayed flagrantly, if one needs to climb the corporate (or any) ladder for that matter.

In reality, they handle these two qualities quite uniquely. I can vouch for thousands of my former students who have done satisfyingly well in their professions, but wouldn't have got where they are so rapidly, if not for ambition and a degree of competitiveness with leadership competencies. These are the same students who while growing at work, never forgot to lend a hand to their peers, or juniors, or helping their older colleagues in need. There are innumerable instances where peers or alumni help to find a position in the company with a gentle nudge, or a kind word about the aspirant. I would think this expanded view of humanity can be best explained in the Greek term *philia*[40] *or prema,* in Indic literature. This broadly means concern for fellow humans, and also referred to as *ubuntu* earlier on.

Millennials grew up witnessing the worst of life situations; societies riven with unprecedented levels of income inequalities, higher costs of education, economic downturns, and a health pandemic crowding their collective consciousness. There is less trust and confidence in their country's government and organizations. This is also what unites millennials across the globe. Could this be an inadvertent winning strategy in the survival game of sharing in scarcity as against seizing and destroying all chances of survival?

This is why, millennials tend to shrug off the seemingly patronizing approach of the Gen Xers in workplaces. Millennials distinguish themselves from other generations when it comes to their collective worldview and networking abilities. Have you noticed how oblivious they are and how easily they rise above the stereotypical rhetoric of color, creed, ethnicity, race, or taste? They are more inclusive when it comes to accepting diversity, something the earlier generations

---

[40] Philia is the second of the four types of love described in the Bible. It is love between friends. It is like a fellowship. When philia and the fourth type of love agape intersect it is a type of life long, unconditional friendship. In Indian philosophy it is expressed as prema – the larger love of humankind.

could perhaps never have been able to accept as freely. For the earlier generations, creating hierarchies was a primary way of establishing their socially upward mobility. B-Schools spend hours teaching the subject of organizational politics, with faculty specializing and producing articles dedicated to this theme.

Millennials share a more kindred spirit and generally possess a greater collective conscience; the same sensitivity spilling into the concern for the natural environment. This spirit drives them closer to each other while carrying a notion that seniors have done little to give them a better world. This kind of equanimity between individual ambitions and competitiveness could be due to an entrenched worldview that millennials carry as Netizens. Their exposure to so many different beings and virtual experiences from across the globe, has led them to be more open and accepting. We shall see this elaborately in the chapter on Global Millennials.

In summary, Gen X bosses tend to hold the traditional notion that a stone when polished hard enough could emerge as a diamond. This does not find favor with the millennials.

Millennials team players?

Most of the studies on millennials maintain that they are more team oriented. So much so that they lack personal ambition. The statement on lack of ambition is to be read relative to the previous generations. It is interesting that the Deloitte-Greenhouse report[41] on millennials in the workplace, suggests something contrary to all that has been written about millennials in the previous decade or so. Though the data pertains to American millennials, the findings are interesting enough to be shared. I have been privy to this phenomenon with the younger cohorts within the millennials. I found that unlike their earlier counterparts, later day millennials were less trusting and their ability to tolerate peer level conflict was much less, compared to earlier generations. This proposition must sound counter-intuitive to the earlier statements in this section?

---

41 Deloitte Greenhouse™ Business Chemistry® (2017). The Millennial Mindset Work styles and aspirations of millennials. The survey involved 20,000 workers, across three generations studied over four years.

Some studies have found that millennials while showing proclivity for being socially conscious, are diversity minded individuals. But the more the new research and deeper the studies, more data which is contrary is emerging. For example, it is becoming evident that many millennials prefer to work with colleagues who have similar strengths. This can be attributed to their conflict avoidance and ambiguity reducing preferences among the team. However, they still have a high sense of competition that they keep hidden deep inside. Like the Gen X and Baby Boomers they are equally programmed to do well and seek personal growth in the workplace.

I found a distinct difference among the cohorts of youth that I interacted with in the first two decades of the millennium and their ability to be team players. I rarely came across any students pulling down an individual's reputation openly or ever harming or disgracing anyone. In group assignments, there could be the typical laggards, free loaders, and mischief makers, but never anything more serious to rustle up deep acrimony among them. Team play was always upheld. However, I also found a special tendency among the millennials when it came to eliciting information, to the exclusion of peers.

There was this strong tendency among millennials to being told personally and privately my expectations from an assigned activity, after it had been announced in class. Even a relatively less complex assignment would be met with dozens of questions, with individual students queuing up for clarifications and mind you this, despite explaining in class, sending out emails, or reiterating it through teaching assistants and student group leaders. They would even wish for us to share with them important sections in the curriculum that were likely to appear in the term end assessments. The tendency of avoiding surprises or uncertainty, was more pronounced among them.

This was even more evident during the employment process at the time when overall there existed a much lowered level of tolerance to ambiguity and less belief in their peers' information sharing. Reflecting on this, and accounting for the general edginess that accompanies that phase, I also perceived an acute sense of competition that made them wary and careful of others. There was perhaps the twin existence of the desire to get an edge over the others in the competition, while being fearful of coming across as overtly aggressive; a trait seriously frowned upon by the faculty and selectors alike, that drove the described behaviours.

I am inclined to believe that millennials are competitive as they faced tough challenges in a shrinking job market. Perhaps these circumstances have forced millennials to become individualistic. *Espirit the corps,* team play, is evident only once a team is formed and a job needs to be executed in a targeted time. Preceding that, it is all about the need to make a mark, and win a plum assignment.

As more and more research about millennials is published, it enables us to understand how inter-generational dynamics is emerging in the workplace. This will enable us to understand how the earlier generation/s in current leadership can deal with the incoming millennial workforce. Knowing them better will enable them to appropriately handle issues of stress and ambiguity that emerge while working together.

New evidence reveals they are no less competitive than their Gen X and Baby Boomer counterparts.

INTER-GENERATIONAL DYNAMICS, DIVERSITY, AND INCLUSION IN THE 21ST CENTURY WORKPLACE

A few pertinent pointers are being raised in this section.

For e.g. what were the characteristics of Gen X that shaped the millennials' mindsets and views of life? How have they been raised as children? How were they treated in school while growing up? What was the relationship with technology in their formative years? How ambitious were they? Did they display strong individualistic or leadership tendencies? All these have been documented in the earlier chapters. More insights into how their growing up influences are playing out in their adult years is presented.

As the world of work stands today, there exists a multi-generational workforce with four primary generations — the Baby Boomers, Generation X, the Millennials, and Generation Z in it. The Silent Generation too exists but as a very miniscule section of the total workforce. All sections in the workforce carry different notions about their treatment and opportunities. In short, they have distinct opinions on the work ethic. Ageism has found its way into the workplace and is an important aspect of an organization's efforts in maintaining diversity and inclusion initiatives. According to Forensic Notes[42] 'ageism' is defined as stereotyping and discriminating against individuals or groups on the basis of their age. It is a social construct that either looks at older persons with a negative attitude or has the tendency to structure a workplace based on the assumption that everyone is young.

The word 'ageism' has taken on a whole new meaning where it is not the usual younger generation that cries foul for being passed on over plum employment or growth opportunities, but actually refers to Gen X or Baby Boomers who are denied opportunities due to their age. Author and activist Ashton Applewhite's book, *This Chair Rocks: A Manifesto Against Ageism*, speaks against age-based discrimination from the other side (older folks).[43] Applewhite has been at the forefront in urging corporations to look at people without age related biases. Interestingly, this fight is against tech companies and other *new age* businesses that notoriously promote youth while weeding out the 'seniors' from organizations.

A persistent clamor for eradicating this bias has taken larger proportions. As of now, the bias against age is most inclined and usually associated with hi-tech software driven companies. New age start-ups and tech driven companies tend to prefer younger recruits, facile and familiar with coding, big data analysis, and handling hi-tech gadgets. New age firms also include those industries that set a premium on youth such as fashion, cosmetics, gaming, and school teaching.

The movie, *The Intern* (2015), depicts this age-related juxtaposition well. The movie is based on a sprightly septuagenarian being hired through a government recruitment facility, who begins work in an online fashion apparel firm owned and led by a young, dynamic female millennial. The initial *'let's get him out at the end of the first week'* attitude of the proprietor gives way to a mutually beneficial relationship for the business. The female boss is a typical, sassy, hi-tech business owner and depicts all that a typical millennial is. She is a workaholic, incredibly passionate and driven, and works tirelessly at home as well as at the firm, to get it going. After his joining her firm, within a week or two, this millennial comes to rely on the septuagenarian's tacit wisdom in marketing, overall

---

42 Forensic Notes. What is Ageism. https://www.forensicnotes.com/definition-what-is-ageism-and-age-discrimination/

43 Home Page Ashton Applewhite. https://thischairrocks.com/

camaraderie with the young team members and supportive demeanor towards her. He helps the company's bottom line to improve as well as the efficiency of the production line. Despite his lack of tech skills and advanced age, he is feted for his contribution and finally offered a permanent job in the company.

This story is a case in point to show that millennials have their biases against GenX/Baby Boomers too.

A research study by Kununu[44] for Monster.com, found companies in categories ranging from retail to manufacturing that were not age profilers and some like Franklin International which had employees who were over 70 years old too. It was heartening to see H&M, Nike, and SafeStreets in that list. The same cannot be said of tech companies which have very few Baby Boomers in the workforce. Tech companies are being pounded for biased recruitments that favor youth over experience, especially in aging geographies.

While ageism in the public domain, vocalizes discrimination against older sections of the workforce and their shrinking chances of employment, the millennials have their own gripes. Let's see how it plays out for them.

A SHRUNKEN EMPLOYMENT PIE FOR MILLENNIALS

Millennials allege facing generational discrimination. They are upset over shrunk opportunities, overwork, and stress. They are inclined to research companies' backgrounds thoroughly or even their 'would be' bosses on social networking sites before they contemplate joining companies. Millennials tend to feel that their age impacts the way they are viewed in the workplace and their hiring. In appraisals, they frequently complain about not being given a fair chance by their bosses. They allege that bosses do not provide regular and precise feedback for enhancing performance analysis and improvement. Due to less frequent and precise feedback they believe, their chances of being appraised fairly, diminish significantly. Gen X bosses generally believe that millennials lack initiative and work well only when clear targets and precise instructions are given to them.

---

[44] Kununu – an employee review platform. www.kununu.com

In reality, these expectations are not always possible to follow meticulously in the face of accomplishing stiff goals and targets. Bosses feel that in such times despite millennials being accorded the freedom to perform the tasks, they tend to be hesitant in grabbing opportunities and proving their mettle. One can attribute this to several factors such as their fetish for precision and clarity, their overpowering need not to go wrong and lose reputation, and also to their upbringing. Millennials were brought up with meticulous instructions and *to do* lists posted on refrigerators by their parents and consequently in their grown-up years prefer to receive more frequent and regular feedback on their performance. In the face of deadlines, they tend to appear stressed and confused.

To overcome this relative lack of ability to deal with uncertainty, forward thinking companies have put in place appropriate policies for ensuring that they are able to retain and groom the talent that is coming through their portals. For once, Gen X managers are having to put their thinking caps on to understand their priorities and put together a workplace that is open and welcoming for millennials. The realization that millennials will eventually don the mantle of leadership is a growing voice in the corridors of power.

The Great Places to Work and Fortune Survey 2020[45] of the top 75 companies that are ideal to work for millennials threw up interesting names. The top 10 places had *old economy* corporates -- Hilton (hospitality), Wegmans Food Markets (retail), Kimptons Hotels and Restaurants (hospitality), and Edward Jones (insurance/financial services). There were four information technology companies, Ultimate Software, Cisco, WorkDay, and Salesforce in the list. However, Hilton was judged right at the top for its avowed allegiance to providing millennials an innovative environment, dynamic development and recognition opportunities, exciting global options, worldwide travel perks, industry leading benefits, and a happier work environment. In the earlier editions of the survey, software companies like Red Hat, Cisco, and Hubspot had made it to the top slots. The same survey in India conducted with the

---

[45] 75 Best Large Workplaces for Millennials (2019). Fortune 100 Best Companies to Work For® 2020. https://www.greatplacetowork.com/best-workplaces/100-best/2020; https://fortune.com/best-workplaces-millennials/

Economic Times newspaper on Great Places to Work,[46] had four new age businesses in the top 10 companies rated as great places to work. The trend seems to be a worldwide phenomenon that has realized the importance of attracting and retaining millennial talent.

While these top ten companies could pat themselves on their backs for their millennial friendly policies, exceptions exist as found out by Blind (an anonymous social network), in 2020. Based on an extensive survey of companies in the US, some companies lower on millennials' lists were, WeWork, J P Morgan Chase, and Nutanix (a cloud computing company). Some of the qualitative factors that were cited as the top reasons for millennial disapproval included the deterioration in mental health leading to burnouts. Overwork, excessive partying, and late work were tagged as the culprits for this. Interestingly, some highly reputed companies like IBM, Nvidia, Expedia, EBay, Symantec, and Twitter also found their names on that list. The reality is that millennials have Gen X members as their bosses who have had a different work ethic all their lives. To add to that, most workplaces do not offer mental health benefits to cope with the dizzying routines.

According to Wasserman (2019)[47], 45 percent supervisors did not receive mental health training and there was no mental health insurance. The move away from software centered job pursuits resulted in healthcare and finance industries becoming the top gainers as nurses, business analysts, accountants, and corporate finance specialists became the preferred professions of the millennials.

THE MILLENNIAL PRIORITIES

The early cohort of millennials is in the most important phase of their lives having joined the workforce in the early decades of this millennium. The oldest of the cohort is around 40 years while the youngest is around 25 years. The older are in line to occupy senior leadership positions in

---

[46] Top 10 places to work in India (2015). ET Bureau. See: https://economictimes.indiatimes.com/jobs/top-10-places-to-work-in-india/articleshow/49499505.cms

[47] Todd Wasserman (2019). Half of millennials and 75% of Gen Zers have left their job for mental health reasons. https://www.cnbc.com/2019/10/11/mental-health-issues-cause-record-numbers-of-gen-x-z-to-leave-jobs.html

large and small organizations. The youngest of the cohort is in most likelihood testing waters in the world of work. What is the collective psyche of the millennials when it comes to their work life?

The top three millennial priorities once again are, to make a meaningful difference to the community/society through their jobs, to earn good salaries/creating wealth, and to buy their own house. The bleak economic situation has, however, led to reprioritizing of the millennial asset baskets. Financial uncertainty dogs them constantly, acting as a deterrent to longer term commitments such as marriage, buying a house or other equivalent big-ticket acquisition.

The sustained economic recessions are unable to help the millennial cause in seeking fulfilment through employment, an advantage their antecessors enjoyed in an expanding economy over the past 80 years. For them, they face an uphill task to fulfil their life goals even halfway, due to the dwindling opportunities.

CHAPTER 6

Millennial Leadership Ecosystem - Paving the Way

WORKPLACE INTERVENTIONS MILLENNIALS VALUE

In all these years of being among millennials and having to represent them before different stakeholders, there has emerged an understanding about what they consider of value and otherwise. I have had innumerable situations where I needed to transliterate their positions on a plethora of issues. For instance, I found myself representing them to the management when the two sides were in conflict; to the employers when they felt there was something not quite right with the millennials outlook towards work; or to fellow colleagues who held the belief that it was a lost generation! And would you believe me if I said I even represented some of my rather 'outstanding' millennials to their own parents or partners! At such times it seemed that even their kin wore tinted glasses that ended up stereotyping them.

The general understanding of a millennial appears to me as an oversimplification. There is much more that lies beneath the surface. While there is no denying their external behaviors confirm the stereotypes that have been doing the rounds for over a decade, my impression of them is quite different. This comes from my considerable number of years spent among them. It is an outcome of the countless conversations I've had with them inside and outside the classroom. Presented here is a summary version of the straightjackets that millennials are put into by their stakeholders.

- ***Employers:*** Overall the cohort lacks understanding of what corporate life is. They demand and expect too much even before they have contributed meaningfully to the organization.

- ***Academic managements:*** Student demands never seem to diminish. We have clarified almost everything in the students' handbook, and that's that. Despite the facilities we extend, they keep comparing and asking for more. The parents tend to, abdicate their responsibility of counselling erring children. Can they and should they be our problem?

- ***Colleagues:*** An entitled, lazy lot, low on competitiveness and high on distractions. They do not seem to value the sacrifices made by their parents in giving them an expensive education (this refrain is especially true for Indian and Asian students, where families bear the financial burden of education).

- ***Family:*** Overly anxious about performance, comparing with other students, and dissatisfied with the existing state of all things. Late nights, partying, excessive use of the internet, and neglecting health and studies. Academic managements not doing enough. Not getting a job quickly, or not getting a better one than peers, no fancy designation and so on.

Wading through all these stakeholders' expectations and steering the millennial talent to drive results was a task which colleagues found onerous, preferring the arm's length, hands off method of interaction. Somehow, I could never come to terms with this approach. Being a professor of Organization Behavior and Human Resource Management, Denise Rousseau's theory of the psychological contract[48] made huge sense to me when dealing with the students' expectations from the institution. It meant going beyond the transactional exchange dictated solely by the tuition they paid and the reciprocal knowledge we imparted. To me it felt appropriate to assist them in their transformation. I felt duty bound not only as if I owed it to them but also to the society at large.

Schooled as I am in the western concepts of education and the Indian moorings that I grew up in, when I took up teaching I consciously attempted to bring a confluence between the two systems. In the Indian

---

48 Represents the mutual beliefs, perceptions and informal obligations between an employer and an employee. Psychological Contracts are largely reliant on promises between the employer and employee, with trust being the basis for the social exchange. (Rousseau, D. M. (1989). Psychological and implied contracts in organizations. Employee Responsibilities and Rights Journal, 2: 121-139).

philosophy of education, students joining the institution or *gurukul*, were bound in a psychological contract in addition to the economic contract with the guru.

The guru fed, taught basic and advanced writing and numerical skills, literature, sport and also provided emotional succor to the wards. In addition, he was also instrumental in cultivating among students, the power of deduction and induction, scientific temper through inquiry and learning, and imparting skills relating to specializations such as the physical, mental, and spiritual. The guru was the entity, into whose charge the parents left their wards for a period ranging from minimum 16 years to 40 years.

The guru in the ancient Indian education system was not a teacher but a guiding light. When I took up academics I accepted as my *dharma*[49] the eternal role of the guru, of giving my knowledge and insights, selflessly and without expectation.

In the time I invested in them to listen to their ideas, stories, chafes, vents, and problems, I was better able to develop insights about their psyche and cultivate a deeper understanding of their needs.

Their needs were simple. They looked for steers, not micro-managing. Yet, when they were ignorant about something, they expected us to even solve things for them! They were both idealistic and demanding. They had ample desire to make a difference and to take on leadership roles, but preferred it was not top down but more inclusive and incremental. In contrast to Gen Xers who were always thrown into situations and had to wade their way out, with little or no support, the millennials were different in their outlook. While in the process of executing the task, they needed constant feedback and inputs on whether the process was acceptable. They hated being sent back without detailed and pointed feedback.

---

[49] *Dharma* is an important Hindu, Buddhist and yogic concept, referring to a law or principle which governs the universe. The implication of dharma is that there is a right or true way for each person to carry out their life in order to serve both themselves and others. Dharma is closely related to the concepts of duty and selfless service, or *seva*. https://www.yogapedia.com/definition/4967/dharma

In the course of time I classified these requirements into four categories listed below. Providing support in the form of mentoring, coaching, communication and life goals related to work -life integration, were considered most importance. This meant offering the steers to help them shape their attitudes and aptitude for future leadership roles. This is also what they valued in the mentors, not only when at the university, but also when they had stepped into the world of work

MENTORING

Mentoring is now standard practice and most organizations have mentoring systems in place. The purpose of mentoring is helping an inexperienced or new employee to understand and imbibe the organization's work ethic, cultural and social norms. This could be in the form of a formal or informal relationship led by an experienced, knowledgeable employee and an inexperienced or new employee. It is used as a temporary and sometimes also as an intermittent intervention. One has to be careful in choosing mentors as they inadvertently create impressions upon the young recruit that perhaps become lasting ones.

My experiments with mentoring have had proven results. For example, when a new millennial cohort of students joined the programs, my department was ready for them, having initiated a system of attaching them to their senior 'buddies.' Senior student buddies enabled them to make the transition into the academic system providing the new students an instant informal connect. This was important because as newbies, drawn as they were from widespread geographies and diverse cultures, they could get quite overwhelmed with their new environment.

It enabled the students to settle into the academic discipline much faster besides joining club activities and other initiatives. Student buddies served as their first level of contact. In addition to the student buddies, we had in place, faculty mentors who were available to provide counselling to the student buddies and the new entrants. There was a close-knit grouping of senior students, junior students, and faculty mentors with regular communication among them.

This was highly appreciated by the incoming student cohorts. Not only did students feel welcome and at ease in their unfamiliar surroundings, it also paved the way for a permanent bond between the student buddies with the new arrivals. The different levels of mentoring helped the students in keeping alive the tradition of winning accolades for the university. Students representing the university brought glory and set higher benchmarks for the incoming cohorts. The reputation of the department too grew rapidly, attracting better students for the entrance test every year. The rate of student attrition was near zero, which in turn was a positive word of mouth about the program, and its faculty.

When recruiters arrived on campus, the students who were enrolled in the department's programs were appreciated for their technical skills and also, surprisingly their soft skills and good bearing. In psychological tests during recruitment, students tended to score higher on emotional intelligence. Mentoring played a key role in nudging the students to understand and reframe their attitudes and opinions about performance, enabling them to take responsibility for their actions, resolving personal issues, and moving ahead. The school benefitted from the well-settled and purpose driven student groups, which focused on achieving their goals. The graduating cohorts have gone on to making respectable careers and are a force to reckon with in organizations and communities.

The bonding continues to be so strong that the buddy and the mentee have remained in contact even after leaving the university.

FACULTY BUDDY INITIATIVE

Similarly, when new faculty members were recruited, a 'faculty buddy' was assigned to help with the initiation. A sizeable section of the department's new recruits were millennials. This was a deliberate policy for talent pipeline management followed by the university. Millennial faculty members like any other millennials, tended to find the rules and codes of conduct a bit too bureaucratic and slow. In the initial days, it was natural for them to feel claustrophobic in a staid and stoic academic environment.

Along with other senior colleagues from the School of Projects, Real Estate and Infrastructure Management at NICMAR and later at the RICS School of Built Environment -Amity University, I initiated the system and volunteered to be the 'faculty buddy' for new recruits and younger colleagues to ease their initial months in the new work environment. As one leading the School and a mentor, I regularly set aside time for catch ups and to understand the prevailing pain points from their perspective. In my sessions, they were encouraged to speak up and provide feedback about the system. They were urged to ask questions and I was hidebound to provide rationale. There was a Socratic culture of open debate and dissent, that I had consciously nurtured among the members. Suggestions offered by them for making improvements were taken on board and due credit assigned to faculty. In the event that it was not possible, feedback and reasons were provided.

The positive effects of the mentoring system were that student feedback hovered around *very good* to *outstanding* for almost all the faculty members. Faculty research output was enviable and higher than the comparable university average, student attainment was exceptional, and the overall performance of the school was above average. As a young school within the university, it was creditable that several times students enrolled in the school's programs, achieved the highest student academic merit awards, the most coveted of which was the Gold Medal for the best academic performance among all students in the entire university.

THE MILLENNIAL RECRUIT AND THE COACH

Millennials entering work life in large and organized institutions face a system that appears as large, impersonal, overwhelming, and demanding in terms of work performance. As we saw earlier, millennials need their questions to be answered, openly and honestly. Going beyond the initial phase of initiation, millennials look for deeper mentoring. They want the organization to provide interventions for their leadership development, knowledge sharing, developing their potential, and improving productivity, albeit their way.

Most organizations need to go beyond the initial phase of onboarding, simple mentoring, or culture sensitization. This is best expressed by Erik Therwanger,[50] a former marine in the US, who maintains that millennials are likely to remain in an organization where they find

---

[50] Millennials are NOT Your Leadership Challenge (2017). https://www.youtube.com/watch?v=YXvbFIXJo90

passion, empowerment, and are given a high degree of development opportunities. He compares the best practices in defense forces related to this. Mentoring and instructions, rigorous training, role clarity, equal opportunities to lead, and finally identifying completely with fellow mates and the purpose. According to him, if this is followed assiduously, the likelihood of millennials quitting soon after recruitment would be minimized.

Another millennial, Doug Stewart[51] who was reading and writing challenged as a child and adolescent, mentions how a mentor in his college helped him overcome this retrogressive dimension in him to go ahead and excel in college. The mentor got him to look at himself not as a 'victim' but as an empowered person which made Doug a writer, speaker, and coach for other millennials. He classifies mentors into various types such as worldview coach, street view coach, time machine coach, and stealth and categorical coach. Each mentor has a clear scope in mentoring and is essential for ensuring development. Like Doug Stewart who specializes in mentoring the mentors, a large number of millennials like Allison Osborne, Gabrielle Bosche, and Lauren Hoebee have launched their own coaching businesses directed at millennials to help them set priorities for themselves and for achieving work and life goals.

Organizations need to address this need wisely. It is the external as well as internal consistency of a company's image that could act as a deal breaker if not handled wisely. This generation loves transparency and integrity and is willing to trade short term unemployment in favor of a cause.

COACHING BY LINE MANAGERS

Many studies conducted on millennials who have been notoriously blamed for leaving jobs within a few months to a year of joining, clarify that when they see lack of coaching, they feel compelled to move on. Millennials clearly look forward to receiving feedback on their performance. They look to bosses or team members not as mere information providers but also look for more engagement from them. The highest respect is

[51] 5 1/2 Mentors that will change your life (2016). See: https://www.youtube.com/watch?v=quhcyPpCaSk

accorded to the manager who is technically competent and willing to provide specific suggestions for improvement.

When this does not happen, things begin to go wrong. Studies show that millennials are the most disengaged generation among all. In a Gallup[52] poll the number of engaged millennials in the workplace was a mere 28.9 percent. Ahmad Noordin,[53] a millennial and HR Director at Ulta Beauty and a Forbes HR Council Member, attributes disengagement to the usual suspects mentioned earlier, career progression, collaboration, and fair pay.

COMMUNICATION

Communicate, communicate, and communicate some more! This mantra works well with millennials. Millennials are a generation that received elaborate instructions from their parents. They like being apprised with clear scopes of the jobs and expectations and get impatient if there are frequent changes in the task. They are fine up until one does not disturb them with irrelevant and unnecessary information which could lead to doubts and irritation.

For millennials, dissatisfaction with the boss is a primary reason for their quitting jobs. In the absence of this frequent feedback mechanism that they have become so used to, loyalty to the organization is determined by the relationship with the boss. This is tough for the crop of Gen X bosses because this needs prior training. Quarterly, half yearly and annual feedback is something that Gen X bosses have gotten used to, however giving weekly feedback is something that needs effort to sustain. And weekly feedback is what millennials love the most!

Millennials are communication medium agnostic. They are fine with any mode unlike their pickier Gen X counterparts in the workplace. They are comfortable (at times far too much) with the virtual, as long as communication happens at a timely frequency. However, when face to

---

[52] Brandon Rigoni, Bailey Nelson (2016). Few Millennials Are Engaged at Work. Business Journal. See: https://news.gallup.com/businessjournal/195209/few-millennials-engaged-work.aspx

[53] Ahmad Noordin (2015). Why US Millennials are a Gen – Disengaged. See: https://www.linkedin.com/pulse/why-us-millennials-gen-disengaged-ahmad

face, they desire productive and meaningful conversations. Simply put, they like conversations from their seniors that discuss performance and offer steers. Millennials are not necessarily looking for praise but they like to be 'prepared' with meticulous *a priori* information. A clear two-way communication affords them a chance for course correction and development.

A PLUGGED IN GENERATION IN THE WORKPLACE

Ever since their childhood, the internet has served as an instant gratifier. We have seen throughout this book that millennials are a 24x7 plugged in generation. Social media is a means by which they fulfil the desire to be part of a group and for avoiding feeling isolated and potentially vulnerable.[54] The incessant validation coming through social media as well as the need for in-person validation are a potent combination for inducing anxiety, depression, and low self-esteem while at the same time, creating a constant craving for praise, acceptance, and acknowledgement. Many times, they are misunderstood as constantly seeking validation. Seeking validation is a deeply social instinct and is a means of feedback and encouragement from others.

Millennials will need to learn to break the cycle of seeking validation by being made to understand that periodic affirmation is more productive compared to being overly focused on doing work for simply seeking validation. What needs to be initiated are wise policies that take into account the need for regular feedback to the millennials while avoiding the perils of offering constant validation. In the workplace, one is oblivious to the fact that millennials are the only generation which received the most attention and encouragement from their attentive parents in their growing years. Hence, this proactive quest for feedback should not be confused with their desire to seek attention.

When my older child was growing up, I distinctly remember the school management adopting a policy of encouraging every child's overall development. Of course, this was a result of advances in child psychology, parenting, and schooling influences. Schools adopted this with alacrity

---

[54] Sherry Gaba (2019). Letting go of the need for praise, acceptance and acknowledgment. https://www.psychologytoday.com/us/blog/addiction-and-recovery/201907/stop-seeking-validation-others

and so did the parents. This was to ensure an equal opportunity to every child to perform or participate to improve personality and confidence. A noble idea indeed to prevent complexes and fostering the healthy growth of children. I recall an incident in the annual gathering of the school, with some amusement.

> *He was all of 7 years, and was painfully stage shy. He was a bit of an introvert and spoke only when he felt the need. Consequently, he was very bashful and hated the idea of facing strangers. However, the new philosophy adopted by the school meant that every child in the class had to participate in some activity in order to instill confidence in the kids. Thus, when the Annual Day celebrated by the school drew near, he was chosen for a tableau which contained a forest scene, among other some scenes. He was given the role of a tree, was made to crouch behind a large cutout of a tree held before him. The large cutout completely covered the tot, as you may have visualized him discreetly positioned in the second row of tree holders in the back, safely away from any prying human eyes. In short, a highly insignificant part to play. Needless to say, it suited him and he was only too happy that the huge tree he held covered him completely and to his added relief, there were no lines to speak!*

To this day I wonder how much that teeny weeny effort has made a difference to him or for that matter all those children who were given bit roles to overcome stage fear and shyness. Another question begs answering is that were these attempts to satisfy the egos of the Gen X/ Baby Boomer parents to see their wards on stage and perhaps brag about it later? While the memory is still fresh in my mind, I could bet a few dollars my son will not remember his outstanding role of a tree that was supposed to leave everybody mesmerized, and not to forget the central role it has played in improving his confidence and communication skills!

Overlooking the tongue in cheek of the situation described above, this was a far cry from my childhood when teachers scanned talent with rigorous sample auditions, followed by even more rigorous rehearsals before being allowed to perform before an audience. I remember, after the performance, when we took the bows and were applauded, we felt a distinct sense of having achieved something significant and the 'crown' on our heads seemed justifiable.

With the new educational value systems in place, my son like scores of kids at that time, received the 'participation' trophy as against a trophy for a 'meritorious performance' that was the wont in the time of Gen Xers.

To my mind and unbeknownst to them such incidents were the forerunners of the way the millennials would expect to seek recognition.

A NEW KID ON THE BLOCK – WORK-LIFE INTEGRATION

Millennials are more willing to find fulfilment in their jobs and careers through work-life integration. This new term is notches higher in its meaning than the earlier term of work-life balance coined during the time of Gen X/Baby Boomer managers. Gen X leaders have struggled throughout their professional life trying to balance work and their personal or family lives. All was well in corporate land until, in walked the millennials with an idea that sounded too good to be true, demanding work-life *integration*[55]'.

The Gen Xers/ Baby Boomers introduced the term work-life balance because it was natural and expected that it was only hard work and being around for the organization perennially is what would ensure the move to the corner office or upward to the higher floors. For aspirational Gen Xers/ Baby Boomers hard work was ingrained and synonymous with loyalty to the organization. We were subconsciously schooled in this thought by our parents and then in our learning and working environment. Personally, when employed, I remember spending no less than a 10-12-hour work day, working on weekends, and foregoing vacations.

Gen Xers were prepared for work-life with axioms like *Eight to late* and *Nine to never* as representations of tacit approvals for the long working hours. In Japan, Baby Boomers and Gen X workers even died of *karoshi* which was a whole new word that got added to the Japanese dictionary, meaning *death by overwork*. Thousands of people died in

---

[55] Work/Life Balance evokes a binary opposition between work and life. Work/Life Integration is an approach that creates more synergies between all areas that define "life": work, home/family, community, personal well-being, and health. https://haas.berkeley.edu/human-resources/work-life-integration/

Japan due to overwork in the act of showing their undying loyalty to their organizations.

A major part of the discussion on work-life integration also involves how much time the millennial men and women can give to their household and family chores. A study by Pew Research (2017)[56] found that 78 percent women were working 50 weeks per year on average as compared to 72 percent in 2000. However, 49 percent of the women had to look after household work along with their professional work, compared to only 19 percent of the men. There is a growing voice for more egalitarianism and overcoming institutional constraints that restrict women from being treated on par in the workplace and at home.

All over the world, the average work week has increased. Survey conducted by Manpower Group in 2015 found that the worst hit is India, with an average of 52hour weeks and other Asian countries like China. Many countries like USA, Japan, and Brazil have seen an average increase of 5 hours to the existing 40 hours workweek. Some countries like UK and Australia have had relatively smaller average increases of about an hour. Though the data is relatively old, it does point to the sanguine after effects of the 2008 GFC on the millennials' work lives.[57] In obvious terms, there are going to be many changes that the world is bound to witness when it comes to the increased clamor for work-life integration in organizations all around the globe. Radical rethinking and reframing are foreseen as families, communities, and institutions around the world rise to sort out the problems of balancing their roles at work and in families, communities and societies.

Millennials hold a different view wanting more out of life and work not as an unequal, either/or possibility, but as something that would be a natural progression in their lives. In response to this progressive thought, organizations could respond with the introduction of work-life integration.

---

[56] Richard Fry (2018). Young adult households are earning more than most older Americans did at the same age. https://www.pewresearch.org/fact-tank/2018/12/11/young-adult-households-are-earning-more-than-most-older-americans-did-at-the-same-age/

[57] Young Indians clock more hours than global peers (2015). https://www.ndtv.com/business/young-indians-clock-more-work-hours-than-global-peers-survey-1415246

WORKPLACES HAVE MORE WOMEN PARTICIPATING

Workplaces are diverse but not as much as one would like to see them. The Global Gender Gap Report of 2008[58] held that despite some countries improving the index on education and healthcare for women, much remained to be achieved in relation to making organizations completely devoid of discrimination. Improvements in education resulted in women stepping into the mainstream and taking up jobs. It is over a decade, since the first report warned that it would be another 100 years before true gender parity is achieved in the world. The World Economic Forum in 2020 continued on the same somber note of cautioning the world and quantifying the economic losses the world faced as a result of women not being fully and fairly represented in the employment ecosystem. The implications of gender inequalities are enormous when it comes to growth, competitiveness, and future-readiness of economies and businesses.[59] Women need to have more participation in all walks of life. When one speaks of pipeline management for women, one does see a growing number of school and college enrolments among girls as compared to earlier decades. The SDG Goal Nos. 4, 5 and 8[60] are being complied by countries having put together schemes to encourage girls to complete their education and join the workforce. However, there remain massive issues in the provision of an ecosystem for their smooth transitioning to the workplace.

Women millennials have mindsets that Gen Xers/Baby Boomers are perhaps not clued into enough. One notion that is widely prevalent among millennials is that one's gender is no longer a determinant of career growth; a notion inherited from ambitious parents and persistent gender equality activism over decades. This where Sheila's story holds good even more!

Moreover, the meaning of gender as limited to just 2 or 3 types has given way to a variety of choices for individuals. The gender discussion in the new millennium has moved beyond the male and female. Gender today

---

[58] Report, the Global Gender Gap (2008). World Economic Forum, Geneva, Switzerland.

[59] World Economic Forum (2020). https://www.weforum.org/events/world-economic-forum-annual-meeting-2020

[60] UN Sustainable Development Goals. SDG 4 – Quality Education; SDG 5 -Gender Equality; SDG 8- Decent Work and Economic Growth https://www.un.org/development/desa/disabilities/envision2030.html

hovers more in the space of an orientation and identification than the physical especially for women. It is more a mind game of being seen as an equal and not what one is born with. This has resulted in greater complexity in diversity and inclusivity programs related to gender in workplaces.

To add to this in many countries public policy has responded to include expanded gender notions by introducing other options than the traditional binary genders dictated by physiology.

OF MILLENNIAL WOMEN AND MILLENNIAL MEN

Millennial women are as educated as their male counterparts. There still exists a salary gap though it is less than in the earlier generations to the extent of about 15- 20 percent. Overall, there is less inequality in the large metro cities such as New York, Hong Kong, Singapore, and London, where women may earn even more on average than their male counterparts. There are exceptional cases but limited only to industries like finance, business, and professional services. As compared to their Gen Xer/Baby Boomer counterparts in the workplace, millennial women command higher salaries. However, across generations there exists a higher likelihood where millennial women are likely to be without a job and facing poverty despite their more of them having a college degree, as compared to their male counterparts. This makes it even more difficult for them to pay their educational loans.

Millennial women view themselves entirely in contrast to the Gen X and Baby Boomers when it comes to the workplace. Gender inequalities were tolerated by the earlier generations, because of the belief that most of those in employment were not the major wage earners. Millennial women are far more self-confident, desirous of taking charge of their careers, and expect feedback on how they could achieve their objectives. Despite this enthusiasm in fulfilling their leadership goals, millennial women still face challenges in getting there. The findings of a study by Pew Research,[61] on the obstacles millennial women face in being accepted in leadership positions, throws light on the views held by both

---

[61] Pew Research Report (2015). Chapter 3: Obstacles to Female Leadership. See: https://www.pewsocialtrends.org/2015/01/14/chapter-3-obstacles-to-female-leadership/

genders. Both the genders felt that in general it was easier for men to have better opportunities compared to women and this needed to change. Interestingly when it comes to holding high offices, women are held to higher standards compared to men. This leads to a feeling that women would need to possess and prove they have far more qualities and consistency to be considered for the top spots, compared to men. Reading between the lines, it could also mean that businesses may hesitate to hire women for top executive positions.

However, among the more developed economies there are more incidences of millennial women holding managerial positions, as compared to men. This is a good sign though it leaves women with less time to run their homes and time for themselves. Millennial women report having health issues, which means that they are either obese as they do not find time to exercise, or that they suffer from mental health issues on a regular basis. Another fall out of the stress millennial women undergo is the tendency of women to indulge in binge drinking several times a month, unlike their older counterparts.

RECOGNITION ISSUES

Like their older counterparts, millennial women believe that there are huge issues around being recognized. The predominant perception among women millennials is that they have to work disproportionately harder for titbits of praise.

Many reading this will be surprised that physical appearance, mannerisms, and all things that otherwise go unnoticed when it comes to men, are keenly observed and commented upon in workplaces when it comes to women. This unnecessary attention to something as insignificant as what one wears and whether there's make up on one's face or not, continue to endure since the times of the Baby Boomers/ Gen X women stepping into the workplaces. Female millennials are less likely to take this kind of treatment in their stride. Many don't even hesitate to quit jobs and seek employment elsewhere, where the treatment is more at par and above reproach when it comes to inclusivity.

HARRIED, OVERWORKED WOMEN MILLENNIALS

I mentioned earlier how women millennials find it difficult to balance work and life due to longer hours at work. This situation has its effects on their personal lives. More and more millennial couples are known to postpone children because of the long hours and poorer wages which makes child bearing and rearing difficult and challenging.

According to Kathleen Gerson,[62] professor of sociology, the twin pressures of doing well at work and being a devoted parent, giving care to the child and just 'being there', is the core of millennial women's desires. She, therefore, urges organizations to combine equitable partnerships for women to have fulfilling careers and be ideal parents. All organizations should offer more suitable options to their millennial women employees to choose the best fit according to their circumstances.

I recall the case of Abin and Vinnie, the quintessential millennial couple and how they viewed their own work-life issues.

> *Abin, a former student of mine and Vinnie are millennials. Both belong to financially sound families. Their extended families too are highly educated and served in government departments or worked in multinational corporations. Abin had enrolled for a master's degree straight after graduation to improve his prospects of getting a decent job. The job market was extremely competitive and Abin wanted the best for himself. At the same time, Vinnie decided to first get work experience before adding to her bachelor's degree. Both were highly ambitious and got admission in reputed institutions. They had met at a mutual friend's place for an impromptu party and kept up a steady relationship after that.*
>
> *Both entered the workforce with definite ideas of first stabilizing and growing their careers. To this end, Vinnie opted for some international assignments that kept her away from Abin. After a few years, they decided to wed. Once together, their priorities were to give time to themselves, to travel the world, undertake adventure expeditions, and visit exotic destinations. Both agreed that they wanted their we time away from their demanding jobs*

62 Kathleen Gerson (2011). The unfinished revolution: Coming of age in a new era of gender, work, and family. Oxford University Press.

and hectic lifestyles. 'We want to make the best and most unique memories for ourselves,' they loved telling their friends. In the meanwhile, both continued their hectic lives, touring for work and spending only quality time together.

Both had jobs in leading multinational corporations and took home fat pay checks. They held high positions in the companies they worked as a result of consistently high performance. Lately however they've been thinking differently. Abin who is 35-years-old and Vinnie 34, have started questioning how much further they would like to delay an addition to their family.

The couple wants to have children and has been reaching out to others, who like them, chose late parenthood for themselves. Having witnessed the difficulties and tough experiences of a few close relatives who had delayed child bearing, they are now serious about taking an earlier call for themselves. One of the reasons was the experience of their 'Mobys' relatives who were finding it difficult to keep up with the indefatigable energy of their little kids and the constant attention they demanded. Abin and Vinnie have come to the conclusion that it would be wiser not to delay any further.

Abin shared with me that Vinnie and he were at a loss as to how Vinnie would cope with her long hours and responsibilities at work and while raising a normal healthy child.

It seems that in the new millennium, millennial women are caught between the devil and the sea. They are highly qualified alpha women, socially aware, driven to make a difference, however are met with resistance and face dead ends due to structural, economic and social roadblocks they encounter. Public policy and organizations need to take note of this and strongly implement the UN Sustainable Develop Goals related to women development.

CHAPTER 7

Millennials Across the World

The word millennial largely originated in the US, though now it is used in fairly generic terms across the globe. One also agrees that no two millennials are alike, there is a good degree of variance within cohorts as well as between individuals. In the case of the latter there could be individuals who may not respond to the typical description of millennials that one knows as being 'lazy, entitled, biased, and legacy driven.' Others may fit the description more closely. Interestingly, even within the cohort there are differences, with the earlier, middle, and later millennials showing different characteristics. The younger millennials exhibit few characteristics akin to Gen Z while the older, to Gen X.

Despite, or perhaps because of this, millennials continue to grab the headlines. And with good reason: In the US alone, there are 83.1 million millennials, according to the Census Bureau. Compare that to 75.4 million Baby Boomers, who have been displaced from the headlines by this younger generation. According to the Financial Times,[63] of the 7 billion people worldwide, 35 percent or 2.45 billion are millennials, making them the largest generation alive. India is home to an estimated 700 million millennials; China, 415 million; and Latin America, 176 million.[64], [65]

It is also generally assumed that millennials outside the USA have distinct

---

63 Cale Tilford (2018). The millennial moments: in Charts. https://www.ft.com/content/f81ac17a-68ae-11e8-b6eb-4acfcfb08c11

64 Catalyst, *Quick Take: Generations—Demographic Trends in Population and Workforce* (November 7, 2019). https://www.catalyst.org/research/generations-demographic-trends-in-population-and-workforce/

65 Asian Millennials: the new big spenders in the Asian Markets (2017). https://www.huffpost.com/entry/asian-millennials-the-new_b_12937942

cultural moorings and defining events at the national level that have shaped them into being what they are. Recent studies show that despite increased globalization and redefining global events such as the economic meltdown of 2008 and the COVID-19 pandemic of 2020, national socio-eco-cultural dynamics and events have a fairly large bearing on the way millennials in the rest of the world view their lives and their future. Having said that country level priorities carry significant importance, there continues to exist massive connectedness to global causes that keep millennials in solidarity. In fact, millennials across the world increasingly identify and reach out to fellow millennials facing difficulties in other countries. They are definitely not as insular as the earlier generations had been on matters such as environment for instance.

Millennials in Europe, North America, Asia, Africa and Middle East and North Africa (MENA), and other parts of the world appear, simultaneously similar and different from typical American millennials. One knows that the largest number of millennials are in Asia. India and China separately have a greater number of millennials than the entire population of the United States.[66] In the European Union the millennial population is less than the Baby Boomers which means in the coming decade, there are fewer people likely to join the workforce. An insight into millennials' minds, not solely from the American perspective but for the entire world is of extreme significance as they will soon comprise the majority of the world's workforce.

Is there going to be a percipient change in the way governments deal with the imminent presence of millennials in the polity?

The next section offers a peek at the millennial mindsets around the world and the portentous implications for institutions their growing presence will entail.

ASIA

By far the continent of greatest significance of millennial leadership will be Asia and key countries within it like China, India, Korea, and Japan. Each of these have different stories to tell, in their handling of

---

66 Catalyst (2019). *Quick Take: Generations—Demographic Trends in Population and Workforce* (November, 7).

millennials. Existing institutions in these countries will need to put their heads together in delivering millennial expectations and creating opportunities for them. Millennials in Asian countries respond to the typical American millennial characteristics viz. being less focused, less loyal, self-entitled, delaying long term relationships, and worried about their future, in short as being emotionally fragile.

This is especially true of South Korea and Japan where millennials have reported being so overwhelmed by the financial and social challenges that research shows they have even stopped dating, preferring to postpone marriages and having children. In South Korea, for instance, millennials are called the *3Po* Generation[67]. Some of these predicaments are brought forth in the globally acclaimed South Korean movie *Parasite.* The movie very ably portrays contemporary South Korean society, its increasing class divide and unemployment, the financial difficulties that the millennials face, and the rather desperate ways of dealing with the crisis. This could be true of any country in Asia facing a difficult socio-economic situation.

Millennials in Asia are very tech savvy like their western counterparts. Urban upper middle class and middle-class millennials have been raised as per lifestyles similar to those in the west. Asian millennials come from densely populated countries and most of them do not have the social security net to fall back on unlike their American counterparts. They pursue education, have high student debts and are willing to defer marriage in favor of good jobs, travel, and other priorities. This is most prevalent in India where youth supported by their families seek higher education as a passport to growth. They are doing this because they are high on aspirations and at the same time face cut throat competition not only among themselves but with Gen Xer who populate the higher echelons in all institutions.

Some key economies such as India, Vietnam, and Singapore are performing well with positive gross domestic products. These are high growth emerging markets in Asia. Interestingly within Asia there are differences when it comes to millennial mindsets, shaped by the demographic, economic, and general conditions within these countries.

---

[67] Sampo Generation, reeling under student debt, postponing marriages and children and employed in unstable jobs.

It is known that Japanese, Korean and Chinese populations are on the decline especially the millennials, who are entering the productive workforce. South Korea has had an economic slowdown for some years now. As a result, these countries' ability to maintain high growth rates is under a cloud. On the other hand, India, Bangladesh, and Indonesia are showing increase in population. This trend is likely to continue till 2030. Countries like Bangladesh, Indonesia, and India will have declining population by 2050, however, Nigeria's rapidly rising population growth rate is estimated to overtake that of these countries.

The kind of phenomenon that India, Bangladesh, and Indonesia is facing is resulting in what is popularly known as the demographic dividend.[68] Ideally, economists hold that when a country's population is growing, it boosts economic growth and the prospects of employment for the new cohorts is higher. When countries take appropriate steps to boost their economies, the youth is upbeat and has a perspective of life which is more positive when it comes to their future outlook. The caveat is that the employment rate has to be commensurately high to absorb the new cohorts joining the workforce. The very same advantage could go completely awry if the youth are unable to be absorbed in the mainstream.

Due to the positive economic growth, millennials in these countries are therefore by and large more optimistic. They are also found to be very competitive because they know that if they have to rise in the vertical hierarchy, they will need to be better than the others in their cohort. Like the Gen X/ Baby Boomers, the millennials are competitive and most of them would like to take up leadership positions in their careers. They are interested in becoming chief executives and leading their organizations, unlike their counterparts in the US. Asian millennials are not overly concerned with being seen as team players. They place greater importance on working towards acquiring leadership roles, they are willing to work hard and long hours, compared to their western and European counterparts, to enhance their career opportunities while upgrading existing or learning new skills.[69] Much like what we saw in the case of Abin and Vinnie in the previous chapter.

---

[68] Matthew Dobbs (2017). The rise of young Asia: how millennials are transforming a region. https://www.schroders.com/en/ch/wealth-management/insights/markte/the-rise-of-young-asia-how-millennials-are-transforming-a-region/

[69] Henrik Bresman (2015). What Millennials Want from Work, Charted Across the World. https://hbr.org/2015/02/what-millennials-want-from-work-charted-across-the-world

In 2015-19, the highest annual salary increases in percentage terms were in India and China.[70],[71] This optimism is quite unlike millennials in America and the European Union. For the western world, the preoccupation with the environment is higher priority and millennials are willing to spend their time, money, and effort to ensure that governments and corporations work towards the cause assiduously. Asian millennials, on the other hand, appear happy to concentrate on improving their own individual living standards. This could be attributed to the aspirational lower middle and rapidly growing middle class (MC), as also the upper middle class (UMC) families in India and China.

In China alone, the numbers show the growing purchasing power of the millennials. In 2012, Chinese MC and UMC families were only 17 percent of the population, by 2022 they are expected to increase to 63 percent![72] So also the growing middle class in India which was estimated at 53.3 million households in 2016, compared to around 31.4 million households in 2011[73] (NCAER, *Economic Times*).

However, global influences are quite strong and therefore these millennials are not completely cavalier in their views on the environment. They *do* subscribe to the need to be environmentally sustainable, but let's just say that most are not going out on a limb to make it their life's calling. When there is a choice, chances are they will not forego other priorities in favor of the natural environment. Therefore, it is difficult to find huge subscription to a Greenpeace like movement among the millennials in Asia, compared to say solidarity marches for youth rights, LGBTQI rights, and diversity and inclusivity rights. This marginally less conscience towards the natural environment could be attributed

---

[70] Report (2016). Annual Compensation & Benefits Trends Survey India FY 2015-16. https://www2.deloitte.com/content/dam/Deloitte/in/Documents/human-capital/in-hc-deloitte-india-annual-compensation-trends-survey-report-fy-2016-noexp.pdf

[71] Matthew Dobbs (2017). The rise of young Asia: how millennials are transforming a region. https://www.schroders.com/en/insights/economics/the-rise-of-young-asia-how-millennials-are-transforming-a-region/

[72] Alicia Kim (2018.) The millennial experience in America and Asia. https://www.edelman.com/post/millennial-experience-america-asia

[73] Report by National Council for Applied Economic Research's (NCAER) Centre for Macro Consumer Research (2011). Economic Times, India's middle- class population to touch 267 million in 5 yrs. https://economictimes.indiatimes.com/news/economy/indicators/indias-middle-class-population-to-touch-267-million-in-5-yrs/articleshow/7435793.cms?from=mdr

to the rising economic opportunity curve, which promises the millions to haul themselves out of poverty in Asian countries. India leads in its initiatives to do its best in terms of managing economic development with a simultaneous greener footprint through its initiatives like the solar power use, natural fertilizers, tree plantation drives and bio-fuels.

In Hong Kong and Taiwan, the millennials are strong activists in favor of liberalism and human rights. The Hong Kong youth rioted for a few months against the peremptory nature of the extradition bill that was first introduced in April 2019, which held that youth from Hong Kong could be extradited to the Chinese mainland. This implied that the democratic freedom enjoyed by the youth in Hong Kong, compared to the mainland, would be curbed drastically. Hong Kongese feared unfair trials and violent treatment that targeted the activists and journalists in Hong Kong. The riots were brutally suppressed with the police using petrol bombs and imprisoning the protesters.[74]

It is to be noted that Hong Kong has experienced youth protests intermittently for e.g. in 2014 and 2016; however, the one in 2019 was different. This time not only were the millennials leading the protest but there were a large number of Gen Z participating in it. These Gen Zers were as young as 14 and 15 years old![75]

EUROPE

Like Asia, Europe has many countries and there too, one sees shades of similarities and differences among the millennials' outlook of what their future holds for them. The western parts of Europe were the economic powerhouses of the last century. However, post 2008 their gross domestic product has been taking a hit due to global recessionary conditions, shrinking domestic markets, and decline in population. Unlike their American counterparts, millennials here are not inclined to believe that poverty is a result of bad polices, they believe it is an individual choice.[76]

---

[74] BBC (2019). The Hong Kong protests explained in 100 and 500 words. https://www.bbc.com/news/world-asia-china-49317695

[75] Barbara Miller and Brant Cumming (2019). Hong Kong's young protesters face years in prison as courts begin batch-processing cases in Hong Kong. https://www.abc.net.au/news/2019-12-07/hong-kong-unrest-batch-processing-young-protester-cases/11768420

[76] Joseph de Weck and Niall Ferguson. (2019). European Millennials Are Not Like

Across countries however, sustainability is of massive concern. West Europeans, among all millennials in the world, are perhaps the most concerned about the state of the natural environment.

In France, the millennials were a decisive force in getting votes in favor of the 'green' party which introduced more environment friendly policies. They are increasingly moving away from the right and far right ideologies in favor of green governments. In Germany, the rightist parties did not find favor with the millennials as compared to the green parties. In Brussels too (European Parliament), right wingers could not get as many seats as they would have liked. The reason was that the millennials and younger segments of the population want a different style of politics and priorities.

Katharina Schulz is a symbolic representation of this desire.

> *Born in 1985 Katharina Schulz is a 35-year-old Bavarian green activist. She lives by the motto 'saving the world, pragmatically, a step at a time.' She grew up in Ammerse in Bavaria, Germany, and like most Bavarians was taught to live in nature and love it. She cut her teeth in politics as a young activist and was elected as a representative from the Bavarian regional parliament. She can be termed a green politician, trying to bring together enforcement bodies and activists.*
>
> *In the true spirit of the millennials, her views are centrist and therefore appeal to the affluent strata of society. Along with her co-lead candidate, Ludwig Hartmann, a fellow millennial, she is credited with shaping a whole new green politics in the south of Germany. Their growing significance indicates a new turn in Germany's politics.*[77]

Unlike Asian millennials, most European millennials are facing increasing unemployment due to the recession in their own countries. In United Kingdom, the youth are disturbed that the older population controls all

---

Their American Counterparts. *September, 30.* https://www.gmantle.com/publications/2019/9/30/european-millennials-are-not-like-their-american-counterparts

77 Justin Huggler (2018). How a quiet Green revolution is sweeping German politics. Berlin, October https://www.telegraph.co.uk/news/2018/10/17/quiet-green-revolution-sweeping-german-politics/

the wealth and assets while they are facing increasing unemployment and have to depend on government welfare schemes. Their liberalism and worldview have been ruthlessly stopped in its tracks, by the elders who would like to maintain the status quo of government pensions, asset protectionist policies, and higher disposable incomes. The elders hold a majority of the votes in favor of separating from the European Union.

To add to this, western Europe is experiencing an overall decline in population. People therefore, prefer 'being left of right,' expecting the state to ensure that jobs are created while simultaneously migration of labor and refugees within Europe is rationalized.

EAST EUROPE

Having adopted a market- based system, eastern Europe has been reorganizing its internal institutions to catch up with the world's development. Youth are now linked with their global counterparts and are aspirational and desperate to settle into comfortable lives. Like the Asian millennials, they are looking for gainful employment. These countries have joined the European Union at different points in time over the last two decades. Hence, the millennials have experienced life on both ends -- under the erstwhile USSR's hegemony and now as independent, liberal states. However, they are grappling with rising unemployment and higher living costs in their countries. Most of these countries are also very poor.

The imminent pull out of UK from the European Union has spelt another kind of doom on East European millennials. a considerable number of them had moved across to the UK in search of employment. There was free movement of millennials within the European Union which threatens to decrease considerably. In 2016, in the UK, 8 percent of the population was non-British[78] of which 5 percent was European. Of the European population working in the UK, a vast majority was Polish, followed by the Irish and Romanians.

The story of Alina, represents the uncertain predicament of the East European millennials.

---

[78] Reality Check: How many EU nationals live in the UK? (2016). https://www.bbc.com/news/uk-politics-uk-leaves-the-eu-36745584

Alina arrived in UK when she was only 17 years old in 2010, from Slovakia not knowing English well enough to even get by. She was determined to leave her tough world and make it in Britain while simultaneously educating herself in English, a language which would open doors to a better world. For this she had cobbled together some money to pay her tuition fee for a graduate program in one of the colleges in Bristol, England. Upon arrival, she took up work as a waitress in a fast -food restaurant and later became a receptionist in a hospital to support herself financially during her three years of graduation.

After her graduation, by which time she had become quite fluent in English, coupled with her pleasant people centric demeanor it was not difficult for her to secure a job as a receptionist in one of the Big Four consulting firms in London. She began earning a decent salary, with it she rented a two-bedroom apartment in a good neighborhood. She started thinking of getting a master's degree to further strengthen her chances of securing a higher position in the firm. To pay for her enhanced expenses on the tuition, she supplemented her income by putting up her apartment on Air BnB. This way she was once again comfortable in managing her expenses, if not in a comfortable position to generate decent surpluses.

Up until 2018 she was very hopeful of making a life in UK. However, by 2020, when she completed her master's, everything had changed. Alina decided to move back to her home country, Slovakia. For this millennial, UK was no longer what it was when she had first arrived there.

UK had decided to exit from the European Union[79].

Fernando from Spain faced the same predicament, a little more complicated perhaps, as he was also a married man.

Fernando who hails from Barcelona in Spain, was 36 years old in 2020. He was not a typical millennial with an enviable college degree.

---

[79] 17 the names of Alina and Fernando have been altered to protect their identity. These are their personal accounts reproduced here by the author during her visit to UK in 2018.

Barely into his second year of undergraduate studies, he had decided to take off to Mexico, to 'discover' himself. Mexico was a choice that came naturally, as the natives there speak Spanish and the working conditions not so cut throat. His choice of Mexico was more out of expediency as he was neither qualified, nor fluent in English or any other European languages within the European Union. His family was not rich, but had provided a comfortable life to Fernando and his four other siblings. With Spain's economic condition in a steady decline with some of the highest unemployment rates, Fernando did not see any point returning to Spain.

Instead the EU offered him relatively more opportunities of survival. He decided to learn English and made his way to London. To him London was an ideal destination as it was for most EU youth, a global vibrant city, aspirational, young, and full of spunk. He took up odd jobs and finally landed up in one of the hotels in central Paddington in 2014 as receptionist and billing clerk.

In the meantime, he had found a girl and decided to get married. They tied the knot in 2017. When I met him in 2018, Fernando was a much-worried man as UK's decision to leave the European Union had cast a shadow on their future. He shared his woes with me, saying that lack of clarity about who would retain jobs in UK and who would inevitably have to return to the EU was bothering the couple. Fernando's wife was working as a school assistant. Together they earned enough to manage the exorbitant living costs in and around London. It was tough because both loved to be in the UK for the opportunities, multicultural and liberal lifestyle, and access to amenities and entertainment. Both had dreamed of being financially stable by the time Fernando turned 40.

Instead their world had turned upside down.

The stories of Alina and Fernando are cameos of aspirational millennials I met from different countries in the European Union. Their stories are representative of millennials worldwide who possess a global outlook, pursuing the dream of a good life through gainful employment and financial stability regardless of geography or nationality.

MILLENNIALS IN THE MIDDLE EAST (ME) AND AFRICA

When it comes to spending time on the phone, a survey revealed that millennials from in the Middle East and Africa spent on an average 5 hours on their phones every day.[80] This is not too far from their Asian counterparts, who on average spent 6 hours. American millennials topped the average with 7 hours every day on the phone. Geographically, millennials in this region are centrally located in respect of the geographical position and cultural influences from the west and the east, are prevalent in equal measure. Moreover, the countries in this belt, have economic power that ranges from very weak to very rich.

Some nations in Africa or the Middle East are in abject poverty with high income inequalities, while some countries enjoy very high per capita incomes. Like their American counterparts the millennials here too are extremely concerned about the economic situation in their respective countries. Millennials in these countries are of significance because they are disrupting the local status quo. While they are interested in retaining traditional value systems, they also feel that they will not be afraid to change the status quo if restrictive traditions come in their way. This mindset has been shaped by linking up globally with other millennials. Like other millennials they are also always '*on*,' connected to the internet and living the digital way of life. They live life using apps for ordering food, ride shares, exercising, fashion, personal care, calorie and dietary needs.

As revealed in the Ipsos Report,[81] Middle Eastern millennials are ahead when it comes to wearables like the brand *Fitbit*. The highest use of the internet is in Kuwait (88 percent millennials) and the least in Morocco (21 percent). Saudi Arabia has internet usage as high as 79 percent among the millennials. They are increasingly using e-commerce sites for shopping. Middle East and African millennials are becoming increasingly engaged and interested online. They use online mostly for posting content on social media, connecting with friends, and learning about brands and products.

---

[80] Dylan Taylor (2016). From Developed to Developing Cultures: How Millennials Are Influencing Our World. President and COO Colliers International. http://www.brinknews.com/from-developed-to-developing-cultures-how-millennials-are-influencing-our-world/

[81] Ipsos Report (2018). MENA's Millennials Decoded A Glimpse into MENA's Most Disruptive Generation. https://www.ipsos.com/sites/default/files/ct/publication/documents/2018-09/MENAs_Millennials_Decoded.pdf

Like any other global millennials, they are concerned about rising costs of living and unemployment. In the Middle East, they are aware that oil will not last for too long and they would like to be assured that their governments are doing enough to protect their current high standards and quality of life. This is why they want employment rates to increase. In the African region, millennials are quite pessimistic about government policies and their future unlike their upbeat Indian counterparts.

The Arab Spring of 2011 was in a sense a defining moment in the lives of Middle Eastern and north African millennials in Tunisia, Libya, and Egypt. Most of the people on the streets were the millennials who wanted change from dictatorial regimes. Millennials identify strongly with western culture and values and are not very interested in historical conflicts that still dominate the politics of their countries. They are highly concerned about human rights and would like the new regimes to write out constitutions in which women's rights are safeguarded along with human rights. This is quite a contrast from earlier millennial activism. As a result, they desire ardently that their own societies change in favor of liberalism.[82] In the same spirit, they are worried about their future because of rising living costs and unemployment. They are also concerned about the level of corruption, violence, and moral deterioration in public life.

The most celebrated royal in government office is a millennial. Here's his story in cameo.

> *Mohammed Bin Salman (MBS), the Crown Prince and ruling Deputy Prime Minister of Saudi Arabia, is a millennial. Born in 1985,[83] MBS as he is called, assumed office in 2017. He has a bachelor's degree in law from the King Saud University. His interest in politics meant that he started working closely with his father, King Salman bin Abdulaziz Al Saud. MBS is known to have introduced a number of social reforms in Saudi Arabia and also has a different style of diplomacy when it comes to other countries, their politics and religions. He publicly professes non-*

---

82 T.J. Raphael (2014). Millennials are on the rise in the Middle East- and they bring their own agenda. See: https://www.pri.org/stories/2014-07-02/millennials-are-rise-middle-east-and-bring-their-own-agenda

83 Mohammed bin Salman. Saudi Arabian Prince. The Editors of Encyclopaedia Britannica. https://www.britannica.com/biography/Mohammed-bin-Salman Mohammed Bin Salman. https://en.wikipedia.org/wiki/Mohammed_bin_Salman

interference and has demonstrated this in the case of Indian and Chinese Muslims. This is a far cry from the earlier days when Saudi was known to take a strong stand related to Sunni Islam; it is a conservative Sunni Islamic country.

Saudi Arabia is one of the countries in which women have had the least rights and freedom. However, on being made the Deputy Prime Minister, MBS introduced a few significant reforms for women such as removing the ban on female drivers driving private cars, and more freedom to roam publicly, without a male guardian in tow. He came up with regulations that restrict the power of the religious police against the sanctions that are imposed on women. Being a widely travelled person around the world, he thought it was time to lift the ban on public concerts that included female singers and opened the doors for women to get employment in government departments and in private sector firms. In addition, he opened the country to international tourists without prior visa applications and visa on the internet for foreign nationals. He lay special emphasis on technology and has drawn up plans to diversify the Saudi Arabian economy away from oil.

In other countries in the Middle East too winds of liberalism are blowing which include relaxed dress norms for women and their access to education and increased participation in the economy through employment.

MILLENNIALS IN LATIN AMERICA

Millennials make for 30 percent of the total population of Latin America. They have become a strong force in Latin American economics, politics, and societies. Like their global counterparts they are tech savvy and also like the Asian millennials they are positive that they can contribute meaningfully to national development. Latin American millennials show a good deal of alacrity in adopting new behaviors and are not fearful of changing the status quo. Like the Asian millennials they are eager to find solutions to the problems that they are facing. A majority agree that they are instrumental in building their own paths to success.[84] And like most

[84] Fran Mendes (2016). Millennials: the force of change in Latin America. October. See: https://www.bbva.com/en/millennials-force-change-latin-america/

millennials they too are entrepreneurial. Due to their use of computers, smart phones, and gadgets they are increasingly using technology to run small enterprises. Brazilian millennials are the most facile in online shopping at 70 percent, followed by Mexico and Argentinians at 67 percent and 59 percent respectively. They love buying foreign goods.

A massive survey undertaken by the Inter-American Development Bank (IADB) covering seven countries and the Caribbean had exciting findings. Close to 79 percent of the millennials were either studying or working or doing both simultaneously. Approximately 20 percent of them belonged to the economically challenged class. However, even among them almost all were either engaged in some job or were actively seeking one; 79 percent of the millennials yearned for financial independence and stability.[85]

This is evident in the way they carry themselves. They have high self-esteem and are confident that their abilities will help them to succeed in the future. The youth in this region is supported by proactive government policies to enable them to steer clear of the usual traps of drugs and violence that have been rampant for many decades in these countries. This has helped youth develop positive mindsets about their future. Respondents in the IADB survey, showed relatively high levels of self-esteem (the perceptions they had of themselves), self-efficacy (the ability to organize themselves to achieve their own goals), and perseverance (the ability to make progress despite obstacles), which gives them an optimistic outlook of their chances of successfully integrating into a changing labor market.

Like their west European counterparts, Latin American millennials are highly socially conscious. Most of the millennials are inclined towards purchasing goods from socially responsible companies, a sentiment held by millennials globally. They are community minded and would like to do something for society. One in three millennials is inclined to work for a cause or thinks that being involved in community service is important.[86]

---

85 Rafael Novella, Andrea Repetto, Carolina Robino, Graciana Rucci (2018). Executive Summary. Millennials in Latin America and the Caribbean: to work or study? Copyright © 2018 Inter-American Development Bank. https://publications.iadb.org/publications/english/document/resumen-ejecutivo-millenials-ing-web.pdf

86 Mastercard announces Latin America millennial study results (2017). https://newsroom.mastercard.com/latin-america/press-releases/mastercard-announces-latin-america-millennial-study-results/

There is greater participation of the youth in politics and social affairs. This restless generation is making inroads into politics, always the bastion of Gen X/ Baby Boomers. It is easy to spot Peru's Maria Antoneita Alva, Argentina's Martin Guzman, Dominican Republic's Juan Arial Jimenez, Ecuador's Richard Martines, and Venezuela's Simon Zerpa handling economic and financial portfolios in their respective governments and all in the age group of 37-39 years. Almost all of them have studied in the United States and done projects in different parts of the world before entering national politics.

In the 2020 Corona Virus (COVID-19) worldwide pandemic, these millennials had the gigantic responsibility of steering their countries away from the harmful effects of the virus for the people and the economies of their respective countries[87].

Marie Antonieta symbolizes all that the millennials in Latin America aspire and live by and resonates strongly with millennials across the world.

> *María Antonieta Alva[88], Peruvian Minister for Economy and Finance, was born in 1985, now 35 years old. Her father was a rector in an engineering college. She obtained a degree in economics from the Universidad del Pacífico and with a Fulbright scholarship enrolled in Harvard's John F. Kennedy School of Government. Throughout her college life she was active in politics, held student leadership posts and was instrumental in starting new initiatives.*
>
> *She was an active participant in civil organizations. She founded the Coherencia collective, which offers a forum to persons interested in politics. She also served as a coordinator of Ankay, an outfit that helps access full university scholarships to the underprivileged youth. Maria, travelled to India for a stint at Pratham in New Delhi.*

---

87 Brendan O'Boyle (2020). The Millennials Guiding Latin American Economies in Crisis. March 31, 2020. https://www.americasquarterly.org/article/the-millennials-guiding-latin-american-economies-in-crisis/

88 Maria Antonieta Alva Luperdi. https://www.gob.pe/institucion/mef/funcionarios/499-maria-antonieta-alva-luperdi
Who is María Antonieta Alva Luperdi, the young new Minister of Economy of Peru. https://www.infobae.com/america/america-latina/2019/10/03/maria-antonieta-alva-luperdi-la-joven-nueva-ministra-de-economia-de-peru/

She is deeply interested in leadership and has pursued a career in bureaucracy. In a short span of 10 years, Maria rose in the hierarchy from being an analyst in the Directorate of Quality of Public Expenditure and thereafter through various departments of the government which include the Ministry of Economy and Finance, Ministry of Development and Social Inclusion and the Ministry of Education. She has experience of 7 years in all departments in economic planning like programming, planning, monitoring and budget evaluation and managing public expenditure. During the COVID -19 pandemic Maria had to take some tough decisions to shore up the Peruvian economy to combat the falling fortunes.

It is heartening to see, that across the world millennial women whether it is Sheila or Vinnie in India, Alina from Slovakia, Katherina in Germany, or Maria Alva in Peru have similar characteristics and do not shy away from hard work and leadership roles. They have similar drives in pursuing higher education, starting early working towards their goals and more ambitious in fulfilling them.

The millennials across the world are what they are - same yet different. Millennials have strong leadership inclinations and it is up to the generations that precede them to recognize this, groom them, and hand them the reins. A fact that myopic, parochial and extreme nationalists could take note of.

Millennials want the world that they dream of and it is the abiding duty of Gen X/Baby Boomers currently in leadership of all institutions whether private or public, to ensure that policies and affirmative action enable them to realize this.

In case one has missed the essence of what being a millennial soul is; it is the fact that for them geography is truly history.

What will be the shape of the world to come? What would millennials look to having as a foundation that would build their new edifice? What competencies should help them get there? *What can be the hide bound duty of Gen Xers/ Baby Boomers' to enable millennials take up leadership roles?*

Retrospection

Millennials were born with dreams. No matter what their economic station in life, their parents ensured that their millennial wards received the best they could afford. The idea of naming them 'entitled and selfish' originates from parents' single minded attention of giving them the best start to their lives.

Millennials initially became the punching bags for sociologists and therapists followed by employers for their outspokenness, emotional stress, and visibly anti-establishment posturing. I believe that the Gen X/Baby Boomer parents' liberal and somewhat hands-off approach when it came to their children's vital life choices involving education and professional pursuits, lifestyle, love and affiliations has affected the millennials in more ways than one. Is it not duplicitous to cry foul when millennials expect and exercise choices that they were used to when growing up? Millennials' attitudes and worldview are the summation of the dominant influences and choices that they were offered in their formative years in their families and not only the macro environmental influences that shape them.

It is as simple as this. It is the values inherited by next generations from their predecessor generation that determine the basis of what they will pass on to the successor generation. While Baby Boomers grew up in frugal times but made it big over their lifetime, Gen X were slightly more better off, as in the case of USA and Europe. So, when the latter entered the mainstream, the continued trail of economic prosperity was unequivocally shared with the millennials they were raising at home. *For better or for worse!*

As an enquiring mind, I pause to think and seek answers to some very contradictory questions that come up when we speak of millennials:

- For someone who is raised in the '*ungreen*' luxury of cars, homes with heating and cooling systems, packaged foods in plastic and aluminum, how is it that a millennial should care so deeply about the natural environment, its degradation and climate change?

- When packaged goods led to a 24/7 supply of food, a situation of plenty as it were, how is it that they care more about large populations going hungry across the globe?
- When almost all of them had generous amounts of pocket money for spending, how did they become mindful donors to causes and charity, to distant lands and unknown communities?
- How is it that despite being brought up in relative affluence the millennials reach out through volunteering to those not as privileged as them, anywhere in the world?
- When they've seen their parents slogging long hours to maintain a decent lifestyle how is it that they want flexible working hours for themselves?
- Why, despite being brought up as relative *prima donnas and stars*, the millennials believe in the power of many?

Why do we today as a society, find ourselves questioning the millennials' every standpoint? Some explanations can be found in the actions of the generations prior. Let me explain why.

Any generation in its prime thinks and acts on universal presuppositions. I remember that Gen X children like me were often cautioned by their parents and elders that the world is not an innocent place to be in and that individual well-being can be secured by competing for the limited resources. A few axioms like *'fortune favors the brave,'* puritanical values of industriousness, being god fearing and self-disciplined were considered sure shot passports to enjoying the spoils in later life. Competition was considered inevitable and helped bring out the best in a person. To survive and get easy access to resources, one needed to create one's individual equity. There was no harm in making super normal profits, it was the reward for one's toil and ingenuity. These axioms have brought us thus far in our personal journeys.

Over a century and half, one saw individuals earning wealth and having a net worth that was larger than 80 percent of the incomes earned by the people on earth. Private corporations grew so big that some of them have market-worths larger than the gross domestic products (GDPs) of entire countries.

In the meanwhile, education taught us to finely slice people and causes that mattered and to focus only on them. It was very typical for a child to be told that one does not have to bother about what others are doing, and to simply control one's own actions and priorities. Especially in the countries where economic development was a challenge. It was, therefore, natural to grow up thinking about one's immediate individual priorities, one's family, one's company, and sometimes one's community.

A kind of parochialism, arising out of intense competitiveness?

All these observations gave rise to generational priorities. The result...? An endless dialectic at the individual and collective level. The bigger you got, the better you were considered. The more the extracted natural resources, the more a company could manufacture automobiles and consequently the more the number of cars a family could own. The more the cars a family could afford, the better the house in far off suburbia it could own. The more comforts and conveniences I desired, the more the number of hours I needed to invest. The more I got, the more I wanted to belong to the exclusive club of people, with higher status, affording private jets/yachts, cruise ownership. The more I could dream of buying a fancy home on the island (perhaps alongwith the island too), the more I needed to hunt for the means for it. I therefore had to get bigger than what I was. The infinity loop goes into endless rounds.

A loop Gen X/Baby Boomers created for themselves.

After all, good parents would always want their children to get the best. so the good parent that I am, I counselled my children over and over again that being Mr/Ms. Good Enough was not enough, one needed to become Mr/Ms. Best. It is in this world of incremental 'growth and progress' as defined by our times in which the millennials grew up.

Somewhere along this path came the world wide web and its spawn - the social media. With that came the graphic and proximate truth about world poverty, the humungous devastation to nature, heart wrenching inequalities which were hidden behind proxies and litanies or simply ignored. The resultant sanguine revelation that for every ton of natural resource extracted, there could never be any replenishment, for every tree felled, there would be decades of barrenness, for every stream soiled, there would be a dearth of fresh water for the people who lived off it, could not but help sear their young conscience. It is obvious that this generation will question the very basis of the prevalent disparity. Their educated beliefs and ethics will make them feel outraged or guilty at the mindless indulgence of their predecessors.

My guess is that millennials will not be willing to take an ostrich like view. There had to be uneasy questions that needed answering; there had to be a higher degree of introspection to be able to justify the means to the end, for the path chosen by leaders of Gen X/ Baby Boomers. In this sense, predecessor generations will need to confront the costs of their single-minded preoccupation with enhancing shareholder value while compromising larger stakeholder equity, that includes the mute natural environment.

The edifice that the earlier generations thought they'd constructed for the next generations seems to have come somewhat loose, if not crumbling. While the millennials joined by their successors, Gen Z, are busy questioning the very design of this edifice.

AN ENABLING FRAMEWORK AS BASES FOR MILLENNIALS' LEADERSHIP EMPOWERMENT

Their upbringing coupled with the information technology revolution laid the foundation for developing the millennials' worldview. The social media revolution served as a catalyst that fueled the spread of this inquiry, across the globe.

The millennials as a generation do not want 'blood on their hands' when it comes to the planet. Their heightened social consciousness prevents them from the single minded, exclusive pursuit of money at the cost of the greater good. They are citizens of a shared economy that has emerged from shared values. For example, a millennial is happy to Air BnB her way into a vacation throughout her life, rather than overwork her way into owning property at fancy destinations. This conscionable person would not like to lock her money in an occasionally used asset, but instead make a greener choice contributing to something akin to a 'world citizenship?' Let us take a look at what a massive cross-section of the millennials follows as their lives' priorities. Notice how their personal priorities are relatively less important compared to global ones. In a millennials' survey conducted by the World Economic Forum in 2019 nearly half (48.8 percent) of the participants chose climate change as their top concern and 78.1 percent said they would be willing to change their lifestyle to protect the environment[89].

As early as 2012, Michael Porter the highly reputed management guru and strategy professor at Harvard had written, "Millennials are more aware of society's many challenges than previous generations and less willing to accept maximizing shareholder value as a sufficient goal for their work. They are looking for a broader social purpose and want to work somewhere that has such purpose[90]."

Some pointers to recognize the leadership genome of the millennials could lie in their temperament and current predicaments, both.

Aim for the Top Spot, Yet Be Mindful of Others

Within the confines of the family, millennials were afforded the best of what life could offer materially. They also got used to being handed over participation trophies which according to psychologists, led to their belief that they deserved a place at the table almost as if like a birthright. They were groomed to be competitive, and they definitely are, although with a twist. They are *'coopetitive'* (a word derived from a combination of cooperative and competitive) made famous in the Game Theory by John Nash. We see the millennials competing with each other but also helping the larger cause while cooperating with each other.

Interesting? Here's how it played out with a family friend's daughter and her classmate.

> *Kisha and Lawrence were classmates who studied in the same college in metropolitan Mumbai. Both had a master's in commerce and accounting. However, Kisha topped the college and university with a summa cum laude. Mumbai, the financial capital of India is a watering hole for all things finance. Not only do the youngsters*

---

89 John Hewko (2018). This is what millennials want in 2018. 10 Jan 2018 https://www.weforum.org/agenda/2018/01/this-is-what-millennials-want-in-2018

90 Dan Schawbel (2012). Michael E. Porter on Why Companies Must Address Social Issues. Oct 9, 2012,03:00pm EDT https://www.forbes.com/sites/danschawbel/2012/10/09/michael-e-porter-on-why-companies-must-address-social-issues/#60efbff2468a

compete fiercely to be admitted in the accounting and finance streams in colleges, on graduating, jobs are few and therefore keenly contested. An entry level job aspirant with a master's in commerce and accounting will easily compete with thousands of others even more qualified like say one with a chartered accountancy degree holder or a financial analyst or even an MBA with a finance specialization. Leading multinational banks across the world like HSBC, Standard Chartered, CitiCorp, HDFC Capital, and Tata Capital have their back offices and regularly recruit young graduates after putting them through tough entrance tests and selection processes.

One morning Kisha was out visiting a friend, when Lawrence called her and announced that he'd cleared a sticky selection with a leading company and was offered a job as a trainee with a starting salary of Rs 25,000 per month (approx. $335 or £245). This was in 2012 when Kisha was 22 years old. She had been searching desperately for a break. The 2008 GFC, meant that the financial world had not fully recovered from the meltdown.

Jobs were truly hard to come by.

Lawrence asked her if she was okay with taking a shot at it. Normally Kisha would have consulted her parents with whom she lived, before applying. This time, however, with very little time on hand due to the 'walk in' selection process, she decided to land up at the company's doorstep, to try her luck. Throughout the journey from her friend's place to the company, Lawrence briefed her about the tests, the type of general aptitude questions she should expect, the personal interview with the floor manager and team leader, the technical aspects of her finance and accounting subjects, and her overall personality and leadership orientation.

Kisha appeared for the selection, cleared it, and was given the offer right away. She produced her e-certifications and documents, completed all the formalities and headed home to announce her spoils. Her family was happy that she'd winged her way to success. However, over dinner her mother asked, "Tell me Kisha, Lawrence and you have been good friends, as are all in the group of friends you belong. How came he did not tell you earlier that there were vacancies? That way, you and some others in the group could have all tried together and perhaps would had been better prepared?"

Kisha was surprised by her mother's observation, she retorted that it hardly mattered now that she'd cracked the difficult bit. Secretly though she did wonder what Lawrence's motive could have been in delaying the information about the job opening. Was it because he feared that Kisha with her solid academic record and remarkable personality would be a natural choice for the selectors' over him? At the same time, as good friends, he felt he needed to share the information (being cooperative) albeit only after he had secured his position first (being competitive)?

When at the university, I made use of this tendency of the millennials to compete keenly with peers as well as cooperate with the objective to improve their overall performance. I worked hard on devising assignments that brought out an individual's strengths, while simultaneously making them work in groups to improve team work and cooperation. When campus recruitment season commenced every year, a system was devised whereby individuals who cleared the process and secured job offers first were available to coach and share their experiences with the rest of the class. The idea was 'Each One, Help One,' and 'One for All, All for One.' This way the relatively challenged students were assigned a classmate for individual attention, albeit only after the successful classmate had secured his/her own recruitment. Throughout this period the whole class participated in a game of competition and cooperation. In other words, *coopetition.*

The result was that the rate at which the students enrolled in programs in my School, year after year were recruited at a much faster pace, compared to where individuals were mostly lone rangers.

Work Hard but Gain Less Wealth

The millennials are a generation that works for the least returns despite being the most educated, despite being subjected to huge stress in the workplace. This is a strange dichotomy when viewed in the context of how their predecessor generations could garner more wealth with comparatively lesser qualifications. Throughout history there has been a fairly high correlation between higher economic and social attainments with higher levels of education. It is no secret that a college graduate has a far better chance of doing well in life as compared to a college drop out.

Being hit by recession upon recession, the millennials struggle to retain current jobs with little time to aspire and progress towards career advancement. Rising unemployment around the world as well as the simultaneous rise in unwilling gig working has resulted in a fragmented adult working population of alarming proportions, numbers like these seen only during the Great Depression of 1929.

It is a gloomy truth that those who slept in soft beds in their parents' homes in childhood, wake up to hard realities in their shared and cramped accommodations in big cities. For millions of millennials their fairy tale upbringing has met with an abrupt and rude end and most times landed them back into their parents' homes. Strange realities.

A lot will need to be done to ensure that millennials are given a chance to showcase their talent and convert these into competencies. Valuable time is being lost in passing on the mantle, and more delay could mean we have lost the potential of a whole new generation.

An Overwhelming Affiliation to Global Causes

More and more millennials run the risk of landing on their parents' doorstep or making a beeline for social security yet strangely do not seem to give up their loyalty to causes they hold dear. Their priorities continue to remain in favour of making this a better and a more equitable world. A world where there is place for everybody to grow, where their pets will enjoy equal rights as their owners, and where flora and fauna too will appeal for protection against brutal assault, in human courts. A world where no matter what your ideology, background, skin type, or country of origin, there will be access and equality for all.

The current state of the millennials couldn't have been expressed better as was by the *New Yorker*. It said "(*millennials*), *A generation has inherited a world without being able to live in it*". Has this dichotomy of a better life as children and the adult (relative) 'poverty' of their current existence led them to become dysfunctional? The same article carries a quote by sociologist Jean Twenge in which she dramatically declares, "*(Millennials) believe that every job will be fulfilling and then can't even find a boring one. They must lower their expectations and dim their glittering self-images in order to become functional adults*[91]."

Millennials however are far too confident and not likely to succumb to callous policies of organizations. Millennials have voted with their feet and walked out of companies where they find existing leadership does not meet expectations.

Leadership with Empathy

Gone are the days of top down, one sided communication. Millennials want circular dialogues and prefer flat organization structures over titles. This orientation is not altogether misdirected as work is now more and more team based, globalization and diversity are an inherent feature of the firm and retaining skilled talent imperatives for success. In the year 2020, at the peak of the COVID 19 pandemic, the leading real estate developer Emaar, in the ME region, based out of Dubai, abolished all titles including that of the Chairman[92]. The difficult times of the pandemic was used to alter the company's organizational culture described as a *"team of great pooled talent"*, keeping in mind the positive future impact for the next generation employees. The idea is to make every individual in the company empowered and willing to contribute. Perhaps this would resonate with what millennials find singularly engaging about Elon Musk. Musk's idiosyncratic corporate mantra hinges on making progressive and futuristic products, are with the intent to help make the world a better place, and declares so an unbounded emotion. Tesla is the dream choice for practically any millennial in the world who knows its philosophy.

That a kinder world be built urgently is the cause millennials uphold and are ready to fight for (non-violently) and also rise above personal priorities. A huge aside of predecessor generations that had left kindness to charities, non-governmental organizations, and public trusts

---

[91] Jia Tolentino (2017). Where Millennials come from: And why we insist on blaming them for it. November 27, 2017 https://www.newyorker.com/magazine/2017/12/04/where-millennials-come-from

[92] Emaar's Mohamed Alabbar eliminates job titles of all staff. Staff report, 21/07/2020. Khaleej Times. https://www.msn.com/en-ae/news/other/emaars-mohamed-alabbar-eliminates-job-titles-of-all-staff/ar-BB1705dU

has suddenly gone mainstream. For predecessor generations, their overarching concern was to think about the well-being of their families and firms'. The best anyone was willing and could do was to set aside benevolent funds for the needy and disadvantaged. The millennials go much further in their thoughts, they see a whole new world based on far more income equality, social equality, free thought and expression, and a much kinder and sustainable view of the whole world.

They are a hopeful, optimistic generation, thinking that past wrongs will be righted by progressive governments. To that end, some have even plunged into active politics to save the planet. This is best summarized by Alexandria Ocasio-Cortez, "*There is space for change, there is space for justice.*" Ocasio-Cortez is a Democrat millennial who serves as US representative in the 14th Congressional District of New York and who ran for office on the famous 'Green New Deal.' She seems like a personification of all things equitable, global, green, and kind.

THE BACKDROP TO JUMPSTART THE MILLENNIAL LEADERSHIP GENE

The World Economic Forum calls for the world business not to lose the chance it has to impress and woo the highly accomplished and bright sparks in this generation. I propose creating an ecosystem of 'Creating Shared Values.' Organizations need to project their genuine commitment to ecology, equality, wellness, and well-being, much before they advertise for talent. When for example, Nestle, changed its business purpose to becoming a nutrition company rather than a food company, the social and business purpose unified.

In another case, when the US erupted against police brutality meted out to black people, the whole world rose in one voice to condemn the violence. The one voice was predominantly from the millennials of all races. As soon as Amazon, Walmart, and other Fortune 500 companies took a stand that they were happy to lose racist customers and supporting Black Lives Matter movement, they followed it up by removing the relevant merchandise. The result, a positive thump on their back by millions of netizens. More and more, companies that positively affirm the importance of diversity, inclusivity and which engage in solving societal problems will be the first ones to be chosen by the millennials. Not for nothing the millennials have earned the sobriquet of being a 'WOKE' generation.

PLAYING THE PROGNOSTICATOR

In this section I don the hat of a prognosticator. I begin by asking all to close your eyes and envision what kind of a world we will find ourselves in, in the next 5, 10, 15, and 20 years. Yes, that's the world in which the ascending curve of the millennials taking over from the Gen Xers/Baby Boomers will be. That world has begun to take shape already. It is possible to give the millennials their place in the sun. However, as millennials are a product of the way previous generations brought them up, it is for Gen X to decide how it proposes to groom of this huge pool of human talent, while doing so, keeping its heart.... in the right place.

Here is an example of how this has been done by my batchmate, of the Class of '87.

> *Nuwa is 55 years old. He heads a leading international mobility services company in Oman, a European market leader with HQ in Paris and presence in over 140 countries. A master's in business administration, he has carved an enviable career over the last three decades in the corporate world. He looks after the entire Middle East and North Africa region and is also a part of the company's global strategic management team.*
>
> *Nuwa and I went to the same B-school and were in the same class. While he continued to rise in the corporate world, I gave up that life in favor of academics. We lost touch as his work stints were in different parts of the globe. A few years ago, we met at a silver jubilee alumni celebration that got all in the Class of '87 together. While most of us were looking our true age, Nuwa looked as if he'd only just stepped out of B-school! We got talking and he narrated the spoils of his career and most cherished assignment. In the course of the conversation in which I was all ears, he mentioned the 'millennials.' I began to ask him to share more about them. He recounted his early experience in the company. After the silver reunion we met in 2019, once again for a follow through reunion and I took him up on how he was doing with the millennials in the company. Here's his story.*

When Nuwa took charge of MENA operations in Muscat in 2013, he had inherited a company that was suffering considerable losses and found employees in a state of dejection. The average age in the company was around 30 years, needless to say .... mostly millennials!

Nuwa set about putting things in order. The first thing he reworked as a priority even before the profit and loss (P&L) account was the people! He started direct interactions with his employees and team leaders. Soon, he realized that though the team had the required gumption they lacked the gusto, having been beaten badly by the competition. These youngsters were led by their senior counterparts who were passionate about their work so there were no worries with leadership. On applying himself as to why the teams were not clicking it became clear to him that many times the right person was being assigned to the wrong job. Communication with and within teams was tacky and tardy. Soon he introduced a change in roles to match personal and professional interests and skills. For those who were unsure of which role suited them or was of their special interest, job rotation was introduced. Those who were comfortable with a variety of responsibilities and larger team spans were also identified.

Nuwa realized quickly that the millennials had a certain mindset which he along with his Gen X colleagues needed to understand better. He posited to his senior executive team that the millennials must not be compelled to change their mindsets to suit the Gen X way of thinking, instead they as bosses needed to proactively understand the former. He decided that if the Oman operations were to be turned around, and the company to become a sought-after employer brand, he needed to act swiftly.

With the buy in from his senior executive team, he went ahead and introduced a slew of new initiatives which became a runaway hit with the millennial employees:

1. ***Flexiworking hours:** Restrictions on time were lifted and emphasis on networking was introduced. It was held that they were not to be looked at as employees but as entrepreneurs*

who were always conscious of using their time for generating mutual value.

2. ***Ownership and responsibility:*** *Millennials need freedom. They don't need constant supervision and management. If there is a bond of trust they function at their best. This freedom was granted.*

3. ***Rewards and recognition:*** *The company boasts of some of the best rewards and recognition systems. Nuwa knew that millennials were loyal when their contributions were recognized. He introduced various forms from monetary to non- monetary incentives.*

4. ***Communication and Connection:*** *Face to face interactions with team leaders and members were supplemented with Instagram, Snapchat, and Twitter platforms for instant communication and connection. Team members were also encouraged to connect with stakeholders on these platforms for real time resolution of matters.*

5. ***Hiring and letting go policy:*** *The hiring process was a carefully crafted exercise supervised by seniors because firing employees is not what Nuwa believed in. There is a lot that goes into the process of searching and hiring a person with loads of integrity and positive attitude. These two values were assigned the topmost priority in the talent search. Once onboard, the employee is treated almost like royalty. There are no restrictions on budgets when a person is hired. Needless to say, that attrition has been minuscule. Millennials have been with the company for over 7 years in the period that Nuwa has been leading them. I asked Nuwa what happened when an employee had to be let gone. He replied that that moment was pretty rare and if it did come up, it was smooth because the entire process of managing talent had been handled effectively from the very beginning. While working, the employees knew exactly what they needed to work on for improving their personal performance (everything is measured and transparent). Counselling is arranged for employees to first check for an internal job fit, and only then*

> *are they urged to seek outside help. An employee is treated with full respect in the entire process. The company that Nuwa had taken charge of in 2013 had 75 employees which had more than doubled to 185 employees in 2019. Needless to mention how much this speaks of employee retention and loyalty.*

With the might of the millennials behind him, Nuwa turned around the company in the very first year of taking charge. Thereafter, the company has only grown steadily year on year and become highly profitable. The vast improvement in productivity and profitability, has won the company several awards viz. Best International Mobility Services Company at the Word Travel Awards 2019 and an Award for Excellence at Oman Airport.

Since the last financial year, the company has not only become the market leader in its core business of mobility services, but has also strategically started adding new lines. All new forays are with an eye on the digital and 'phygital', keeping in focus the millennial and Generation Z consumers.

The typical popular notions prevailing at that time was of millennials being haughty, unmotivated and lacking strong critical thinking. Nuwa's could be considered exceptional leadership who recognized the millennials' potential and preferences and laid his bets on their leadership early on. This he did at a time when millennials were hardly considered strong contenders for leadership roles in organizations.

Nuwa was ahead of his time and his style of leading millennials ticked all the right boxes. His company's success in a turbulent decade therefore to be a foregone conclusion.

Epilogue

'Times they are a-changing, moments they are a-moving,
In the times and the moments, new hopes they a-creating
New dawns they are a-coming, all lives they are a- changing'

Millennials as envisaged by Howard and Strauss[93] were awesome individuals – caring, earnest, industrious, and positive. The duo in fact categorized them under the archetype, the 'Hero' generation. Somewhere along the way this heroic generation is threatened with blight and that too when it is not necessarily of their doing.

I have always seen in them a naïve yet refreshing outlook towards the world they passionately look forward to living in or inheriting. These quests in themselves, put them into the league of other great generations in history. For instance, the generations in France and USA who died fighting for equality, fraternity, and liberty or earlier on, the Renaissance generation as the harbinger of a modern world of scientific enquiry and technological development. In the nineteenth century the generations in the colonized world led by Gandhi that struggled to free their lands on the same principles of progressive and enlightened polities. All these were generations symbolic of great resilience that preceded even greater struggles to banish the ills that plagued humankind.

This generation is at the cusp of greatness. With digital technology on their side they see a world that I would term as a *Fair New World*, and are enthusiastic to create it!

To make it happen the questions one could ask and probe into are;

What is needed to make this possible? Are companies rewriting their business cases in alignment with millennial moorings? Are organizational structures being revitalized to reflect new thought? Is the entrepreneurial instinct proactively detected and nurtured through better policies by public and private institutions?

---

[93] 'Strauss–Howe generational theory' https://en.m.wikipedia.org/wiki/Strauss-%E2%80%93Howe_generational_theory

By 2025, millennials are slated to outnumber Gen X in workplaces. In such a scenario a larger discourse is needed on what the millennials believe in and what they want. This discourse has to cover public policy, organizational leadership, and academic and research institutions reflecting and responding to the situation. Proactive interventions of these institutions cannot be underestimated. At a micro-level, human resource departments and company leaderships require serious rewiring to accommodate and in fact reload traditional practices in favor of the millennials. Senior managers need to be trained to handle the millennial workforce in a way that they are groomed to lead organizations and institutions, factoring in millennials' priorities.

I reminisce the times I used to refer to Bob Dylan's immortal ditty (I have modified here, at the beginning), when taking classes for my millennial student cohorts, which continues to be contemporary over 50 years on. I referred to the song while explaining the importance of agility of individuals and organizations to change with the times. I also referred to Heraclitus' lines *'Change is the only constant in life'*, ad nauseum, to every new batch that stepped into the university.

I reflected on these lines often but despite my willingness to change in line with their ways, most times, I found myself to be a digital fugitive. Simple actions would send me running the other way. I remained steadfast on my ideas of person to person outreach scoring over the virtual, especially when it came to developing and maintaining, human relationships. In a sense I believe having been a *digital fugitive* did me no great harm. I ended up developing strong and lasting connections with my wards. It's only when I left the university that I began to appreciate how much I needed to catch up, so as to be called a *digital native*. That, I have been fortunate to receive my students' continued love and respect despite being a very late starter in the digital world, is exceptional and humbling.

Nuwa on the other hand was far ahead of the curve when it came to communicating with them, where they were found the most – the Internet. In doing so, he stole a march not only on me, but also on many of the industry leaders who at work, continue being stiff and distant from a generation they had more often than not, themselves raised at home.

Hopefully my fascination with millennials doesn't end with this book. And neither would yours.

Exercises on Millennial Leadership

MILLENNIAL MAESTRO™

Avon's Natural Causes

Avon was suffering from a crisis at work. At 26 years, having received a post graduate qualification in management and securing a comfortable job in a metropolis, all dreams had seemed to materialise before his eyes. He had found his destination. As a kid brought up on small town values of being good and doing good for others, the acute impersonality of the city had initially overwhelmed him. Yet, the values of being accommodative, flexible and willing to learn that helped him in the next six years of his professional life. His boss, peers and subordinates appreciated his team play and the annual 360^0 feedback was easy meat. He was 31 years old and firmly ensconced in his department and organisation.

Lately Avon had begun to feel a creeping discontent related to his work life. Strange thoughts which questioned the very purpose of his life, crept up regularly, leaving him puzzled about his next steps. He began to view things that were *insignificant* to others, as those that had begun to matter to him. His growing interest in reducing the carbon footprint meant dumping the car and cycling to work, or using the metro service. Reducing his use of plastic and other nondegradable items meant being sniggered at openly or covertly by his peers, and friends. His enlightenment towards nature was not always viewed with positivity. Increasingly he had developed a higher level of impatience for the ignorance and inertia of others towards climate change. This was becoming a major cause of stress to him, affecting his interpersonal relations. He thought of doing something about it.

As Avon, what would you do?

Maavi Wants Something More

old. Her job meant covering art and related stories. She had herself graduated from art school with average grades and decided that she would retain her love for art, but not as a career artist. Besides, writing about art would be interesting because it would open up possibilities of meeting great artists and knowing about their journeys. It was a truly exciting prospect for her. Moreover, she was looking forward to the autonomy and independence that the job offered, even though it did not pay her much.

Being a freelancer, she worked alone, making contact with artists for potential interviews, organising the shoots and sending the content for editing to the channel. After that she needed to follow up to find out if the content was being carried with proper edits and high authenticity. She also needed to keep her relations with the temperamental artists well-oiled and was always pensive up until both the artists and the public, received the episode with no fuss.

In a couple of years, the job began to lose its sheen. She began to question the solitary work, with little contact with the team and other folks in the company. She felt lonely and cut off from the action and decision making. Also, she felt she needed to know more about how the company was planning its future and what would entail for freelancers. Conflicting rumours about the company shutting its local branches, trimming staff and introducing pay cuts, was challenged by the company executives, but were disturbing her, she felt left out and lonely.

She felt a growing need to be part of an organisation with shared values and camaraderie. She decided that she needed to change her current state of things.

Is Maavi right in her thinking? What would you do if you were Maavi?

KINESICSORG™

BowMa Millennials

BowMa is a fast- growing AI solutions company located in Bangalore in India with an office in Singapore. It has received three rounds of funding to scale up its operations for two major purposes viz. to expand the applications basket (R&D), expand into new markets (geographically).

BowMa began as a garage atelier when two university friends came together in 2007 to share their ideas for the future. At the time, they were both employed in large software multinationals and were earning six figures pay packages. Meghan then 27 yrs, was a robotics specialist and Nyugen 28 yrs, an IT computation whiz. Both graduated summa cum laude from an ivy league engineering college in 2003 in USA and had received enviable work profiles while on campus. The going was good as they had been given work in the field of AI; at the time AI and ML were growing in significance. Besides at work they were being taken care of well by their respective companies.

However, it was not long before the entrepreneurial bug hit them. They were keen to start their own venture which would be an expression and extension of their work and beliefs. Their ardent desire was to design solutions to alleviate the problems of the differently enabled and the physically challenged people. Finally, when BowMa was formed in 2015, they knew that it was going to be a long and arduous journey ahead. Therefore, they were keen to employ only other like- minded persons who shared their single -minded focus, on making a positive difference to reduce suffering using AI. They began a search for young, qualified engineering graduates as well as hiring from other domains such as social welfare, caregivers, social media influencers and from design schools. Soon they had a motley group of persons working at various developmental aspects in R&D.

Currently BowMa is facing a bit of a challenge. The young blood in the firm with an average age of around 24 years appears as if pulling in different directions. The individuals look at greater degree of flexi-hours, autonomy and independence in their working. This is taking a toll as it was becoming difficult to accommodate individual requests as delivery deadlines were getting severely affected. The highly talented lot, though individually driven, was not able to deliver requisite results. Much hinged on the team performing together, achieving company goals, and delivering stakeholder value. Meghan and Nyugen were worried that the current state of affairs was not going to help achieve their growth plans for the next 3 years and something needed to be done urgently.

Meghan and Nyugen invited Sonia, the HR head for a discussion on how to overcome the issues on hand.

Locking horns at Matterhorn

Matterhorn Ltd was a company established in 1978 by its feisty patriarch, Francois Bernaud. He had risen from humble beginnings working his way from the vineyards of Boulogne in France to become a worldwide conglomerate with businesses ranging from consumer goods, farming, engineering and construction. Francois was a robust personality with indefatigable energy that matched that of a 20-year-old, even as a septuagenarian! His astute business sense coupled with strong people skills had enabled him to become a respected industrialist despite having minimal formal education. One thing about Francois was that he never forgot a favour. That's why it was easy to find older employees continuing to be employed in the organisation. There was growing restlessness and rumblings in almost all divisions of the conglomerate. It was related to people.

Francois decided to invite his scions the two sons and daughter with the top management team to discuss the issue. In the discussion the team came up with a few key observations as follows

- Across the world the conglomerate had 4 generations in the workplace namely the Baby Boomers, Gen X, Millennials and Gen Z. The bulk of millennials comprised the middle and senior management. The Gen X and Baby Boomers the senior and top management while Gen Y were at the entry to middle level. In terms of share the millennials outnumbered all other generations.
- The rumblings were being felt due to certain cultural and professional differences among the generations. The stickiest ones were between the millennials who had older bosses, who, more often than not were

infotech challenged. The bone of contention lay in their stodgy, slow practices and an unwillingness to change which slowed the ability to quickly respond to the changing market demands.

- The millennials were highly qualified and needed to see clear career paths for themselves, there was a degree of impatience towards their bosses. Moreover, the Gen Xs' over emphasis on work, foregoing vacations and prolonging work days in office did not go down well with the millennials as well as Gen Z. The latter had priorities that were not limited to work and the boss' expectations of long working hours, exasperated them.

- They also wanted to be included or at least be heard when new policies were being introduced in the divisions. They often raised the issues of non-transparency during the exit interviews.

- Many millennials felt that the company should also enter into new generation businesses that were driven by IOT and life sciences.

- Employees wanted more engagement from the organisation. Volunteering for causes, like the environment and initiatives for the less privileged was a growing ask from the younger employees.

At the end of the session Francois and his team concluded that Matterhorn Ltd needed an organisational overhaul to reflect the contemporary aspirations. It was time for an organisation wide change management intervention.

As Founder and Director of Vayati Systems and Research, Dr. Mona N. Shah offers her trademark earthy and transformational leadership solutions to build a kinder and sustainable world. She enables individuals, organizations and institutions to rethink, reform and reshape their ethos to meet the needs of a changing future.

She is a multi-dimensional professional with a career spanning over three decades in industry, academia and entrepreneurship. She's at her best when engaged in launching pioneering initiatives and installing enduring systems. She graduated with distinction from Symbiosis Institute of Business Management Pune, in 1987. Her initial stints were with HCL Ltd, Agfa Gevaert, Indian Express and India Properties up until academics beckoned. At the National Institute of Construction Management and Research (NICMAR), she pioneered India's programs in real estate, smart cities and infrastructure management after which she continued in the same vein at RICS School of Built Environment - Amity University. A popular teacher she's been a recipient of awards for academic excellence and meritorious research conferred by professional bodies. Her publications are considered benchmark thought leadership in the areas of management and built environment.

Her career is defined as one absorbed in co-creating solutions for industry and research. She has associated with Hyundai, L&T, PMI, ADB, Shapoorji Pallonji, HDFC Securities Ltd, ABB, Siemens, Tata Housing, Godrej Properties in areas of training and research. Mona also serves on academic, company and non-profit boards and is an invited international speaker.

Her penchant for creativity and innovation, keeps her busy with interests in the performing arts, writing poetry, following nature trails, and counselling.

For enquiries related to bulk orders, and discounts contact

vayati@vayatisystems.com; vayatisystems@gmail.com

Tel: 9910331541 / 7030867656

To refer Millennials - Poised to Lead, to a friend/friends
visit www.vayatisystems.com

"Anyone in academia, commerce or personal life that ponders the millennial mindset will feel better, understanding from reading this book."

Prof. Michael Riley, Pro-Vice Chancellor (Interim), Liverpool John Moores University, UK

"Millennials were born with dreams. This book provides a lens into the world and psyche of the Millennial, or Gen Y.

Dr. Amanda Clack, Executive Director and Head of Strategic Advisory at CBRE, UK. Global Past President of the RICS (2016-17).

"The author has done a good job of capturing the millennial characteristics precisely. This book will serve to help in making decisions in matters related to the millennials".

Nixon Joseph, President & Chief Operating Officer, State Bank of India Foundation, India

"An insightful, highly engaging, and informative read on the "*generational cliqueism*" with many interesting narratives. Definitely worth a place in both Academic and Organizational Archives."

Gopika Menon Nair, Senior Vice President - Human Resources, Training & Development - LALS Group, UAE & GCC.

"Informative, engaging, appealing and not just for the millennials. All in all, an excellent read".

Agney Das, Vice President, JP Morgan Chase & Co. London, UK and a millennial

"We recognise ourselves in multiple aspects and anecdotes, and we also see our parents (as GenX). Mona N. Shah delves into a systematic analysis of the millennial generation."

Rodrigo Bacigalupe, Marta Fratini, Post - Doctoral Research Fellows, K U Leuven, Belgium, Martin Luther University, Wittenburg Germany and Kalliopi Pervolaraki, (PhD), Project Manager, Evotech International GmbH Germany and millennials

VSAR

9 789354 165177